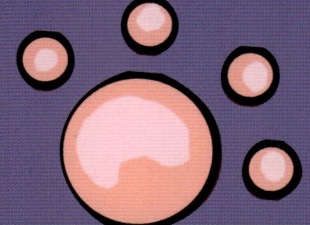

Paint
-a-
Pet

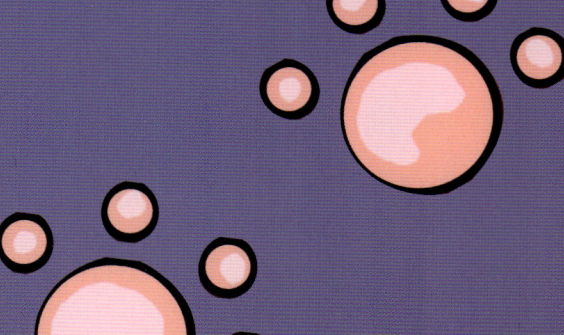

by Linda Gillum

About the Artist

Linda Gillum, an award winning needlework designer, accomplished in pastels, as well as watercolor, acrylic, and oil painting is well known for her adorable animal artwork. Her love for animals is especially evident in this collection of 50 pets of all kinds for you to paint. She has designed them with her keen eye and appreciation for the individuality of the pets we love and their varied purrrsonalities.

She and her husband Joe are parents to two dogs and two cats and are adoptive parents to all the neighborhood dogs.

Whether they are cats, dogs, fish or feathered friends, pets are unique and special to those who love them. Let your imagination run wild and paint these charming critters on your favorite shirts, bags pillows, gifts or home décor projects. Just visualize a border of kittens on a little girl's bedroom wall or a playful puppy on Fido's toy box. They're sure to bring smiles to your entire household. The applications are endless, so start painting!

Table of Contents

8   General Instructions

10 Saint Bernard

11 Labrador Retriever

12 Basset Hound

13 Birman

14 Don't Mess with Me!

15 My Red Bone

16 Pug

17 Schnauzer

18 Best Buddy

19 Boxer

20 Smile

21 Chihuahua

22 Everyone Needs a Teddy Bear

23 Golden Retriever

24 Dalmation

25 Welcome

26 Pony

27 Box Fish

28 Goldfish

29 Trigger Fish

30 Kitty Face

31 Siamese

32 Bunny and Carrot

33 Black and White Bunny

34 Froggie

35	Cockatoo	
36	Newfie Puppy	
37	Yorkie	
38	Poodle	
39	Pomeranian	
40	Walk???	
41	Dogs Have Owners, Cats Have Staff	
42	Puppy Love	
43	Relax	
44	Jack Russell Terrier	
45	Purple Bunny	
46	Orange Kitty	
47	Dachshund	
48	Cat People	

49	Cocker Spaniel	56	Three Kitties
50	German Shepherd	57	Meow
51	Himalayan	58	Spoiled Rotten Dogs
52	Rottweiler	60	Spoiled Rotten Cats
53	Love a Bunny		
54	Love Birds	62	Alphabets and Paw Prints
55	Turtle	64	Resources

General Instructions

Everyone in the family can enjoy painting the fun designs in this book. With the easy paint by number method, you just fill in each area with the color specified in the key and watch your pet portrait come to life. The collection of 50 pets is sure to include some of your favorites. Make them as large or as small as you like for painting everything from a small wooden ornament to a bigger than life image for the wall. The following instructions will get you started.

Paints

I used DecoArt Americana bottled acrylic paints. These paints are non-toxic and water-based so you can clean brushes with soap and water. They are readily available at your local craft or hobby store, by mail order, or online. Acrylic paints dry relatively quickly so you can paint colors next to each other without a problem. Be sure to rinse your brush well in clean water before changing to another color. I like to lay out puddles of paint on a wet-palette so they're available as I paint the various areas of the design. The wet palette will keep the paints moist as you work which is especially helpful if you're using mixed colors and want to keep them consistent. With a wet palette you can also take a painting break and your paints will be moist when you come back to them later. Use a palette knife or craft stick to mix the colors. Ratios listed after paint names indicate how many parts to use of each paint to achieve the desired color (e.g., for Raspberry/White 1:2, mix 1 part Raspberry to 2 parts White).

Brushes

You will need a couple of round brushes for filling in color areas and a liner brush for details. Brush sizes will depend upon the size of your design. I used Loew-Cornell #2 and #4 rounds (Series 7040) and Loew-Cornell 10/0 liner (Series 7350) to make my original pet paintings which were 200% larger than the pictures printed in the book. If you want to paint a life-sized Saint Bernard on your wall, you will definitely need much larger brushes! Rinse brushes often during use, but don't let them sit in a water container for long periods of time. After use, clean thoroughly with soap and water (or brush cleaner), working the soap into the bristles. Always rinse well. When storing, be sure brushes are dry and positioned flat or with the handles down.

Surfaces

Use your imagination to visualize the pets on a variety of surfaces—the possibilities are endless. DecoArt Americana acrylics can be used on almost any surface including wood, metal, canvas, papier mache, walls, fabric, leather, ceramic bisque, watercolor paper (smooth, hot pressed), poster and illustration board. When painting on fabric, mix DecoArt Fabric Painting Medium with the acrylic paints to make them washable and permanent (follow manufacturer's instructions for heat setting) or use DecoArt SoSoft Fabric paints which are available in similar colors. It's easy to find things to paint; you probably already have some items on hand just waiting to be adorned with a pet portrait. If not, you're sure to find a good supply at your local craft, department, or discount store. And don't forget the thrift store and flea market, where you'll find some interesting pieces and good bargains. Use a copy machine to enlarge or reduce the designs to fit your surface.

Preparation

Be sure to prepare your surface before applying the design. Individual project instructions may include special methods of preparation.

Wood surfaces: Fill any holes or dents with wood filler. Sand the entire piece with medium-grit sandpaper and remove any dust. Apply a coat of wood sealer and allow to dry thoroughly. Sand again with fine-grit sandpaper and wipe clean. Appy an even basecoat.

Tin/metal surfaces: For old tin surfaces, remove any rust using naval jelly. Wash thoroughly with soap and water and allow to dry completely. Rinse with a mix of white vinegar + water (1:1) to remove any oil or residue. Sand the entire piece with fine-grit sandpaper and remove any dust. Apply a coat of primer and dry thoroughly. For new tin surfaces, wash with warm soapy water and rinse thoroughly. Rinse with vinegar and water (2 Tbsp.: 1 cup) and allow to dry. Apply matte spray or sand lightly with fine-grit sandpaper to add "tooth." Wipe free of dust.

Canvas surfaces: No preparation is needed for canvas fabric (e.g., tote bags). For stretched canvas, sand lightly with fine-grit sandpaper and remove dust. Apply an even basecoat.

Fabric surfaces: Wash and dry the fabric without using any fabric softener. Iron out any wrinkles.

Basecoating

For most projects, apply an overall basecoat or background color. Keep the surface as smooth and even as possible by painting with a large flat brush and applying several light coats rather than a heavy one. It may take 2–3 coats for good coverage. Always let the paint dry between coats and try to paint as smoothly and evenly as possible.

Transferring Patterns

Trace the pattern onto transparent tracing paper using a fine-tip, permanent black pen or pencil. Trace as accurately as possible. Be sure any basecoated areas are dry before you begin transferring the pattern or the lines may be difficult to remove later (a hair dryer can speed up the drying time). Tape the pattern to the surface in the desired position, then slip a piece of transfer or graphite paper underneath, keeping the graphite side down.

Use gray transfer paper for projects with light-colored backgrounds and white transfer paper for dark backgrounds. Trace over the design using a pencil, inkless pen, or small end of a stylus. Apply with light pressure to avoid leaving indentations on the surface and to keep lines light. In some cases you may need to transfer a design in several steps, starting with the main areas of the design then later adding detail lines. When your project is finished, remove tracing lines with a white art eraser or a damp cotton swab.

Finishing

Remove any visible transfer lines using a white art eraser. To protect your painting on wood, metal, papier mache or other hard surfaces apply two or more coats of water-based varnish. Be sure to follow the manufacturer's instructions. Heat set fabric or canvas if you intend to wash it.

General Supplies

In addition to the paints listed with each project, you'll also need to gather the following general supplies:
- Black Ultra Fine Point Sharpie.
- A round brush and liner brush appropriate to the size of your painting.
- Disposable palette paper (sold in pads) for laying out paints. Substitute with freezer paper, polystyrene foam meat trays, or plastic lids. An artist's wet palette is useful if you want to keep paints moist for a longer period of time.
- Water container, glass jar, or commercial brush basin.
- Tracing paper.
- Transfer paper (sometimes referred to as graphite paper) and pencil, dry ballpoint pen or stylus. For transferring on dark surfaces, use white transfer paper or white chalk pencil.
- Paint mixing tool: palette knife, or wooden craft stick.
- Paper towels to absorb water from brushes and for general cleanup.
- Ruler and white art eraser.

Saint Bernard

Palette
Black
White
Graphite
Neutral Grey
Grey Sky
Slate
Mississippi Mud
Terra Cotta
Medium Flesh
Gingerbread
Raspberry
Sapphire

Instructions
1. Trace drawing and transfer to paint surface.
2. Follow the diagram and paint areas as indicated.
3. Paint large areas of eye such as iris and pupil and add White highlights last.
4. Use Neutral Grey and liner brush to add outlining at end of tail.

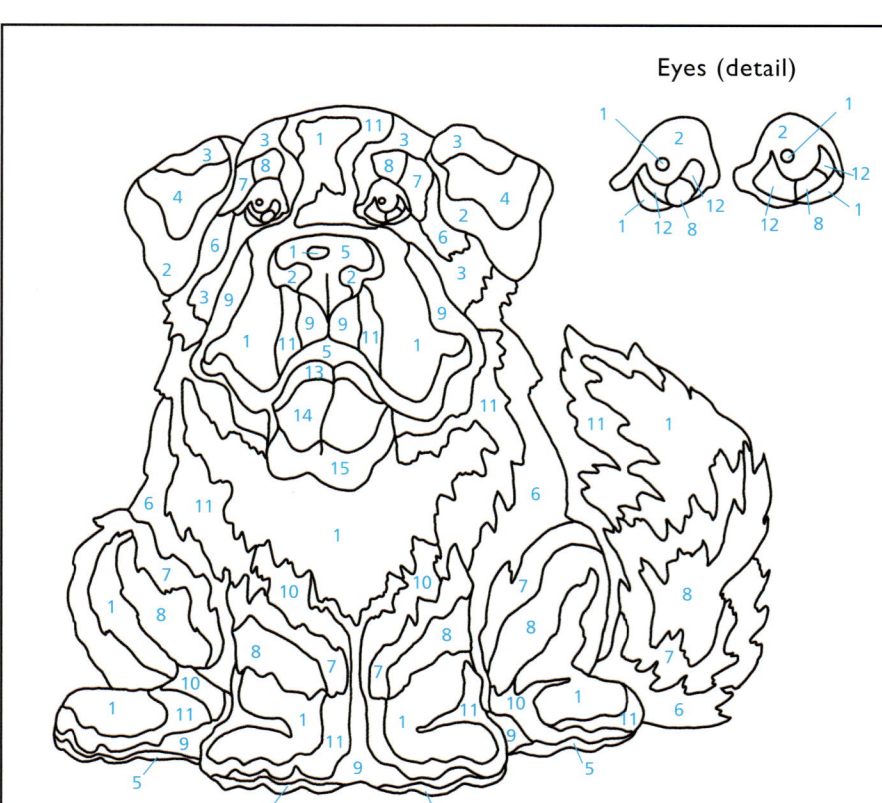

Eyes (detail)

Colors
1. White
2. Black
3. Graphite
4. Mississippi Mud
5. Graphite/Neutral Grey 1:1
6. Terra Cotta
7. Terra Cotta/Medium Flesh 1:1
8. Medium Flesh
9. Slate
10. Grey Sky
11. Grey Sky/White 1:1
12. Gingerbread
13. Raspberry
14. Raspberry/White 1:1
15. Raspberry/White 1:2
16. Sapphire

Labrador Retriever

Palette
Black
White
Graphite
Neutral Grey
Grey Sky
Slate Grey
Light Cinnamon
Gingerbread
True Red
Cadmium Yellow

Instructions
1. Trace drawing and transfer to paint surface.
2. Follow the diagram and paint areas as indicated.
3. Paint large areas of eye such as iris and pupil and add White highlights last.
4. Teeth: dip end of small brush in White and add 5 dots of White for bottom teeth.

Colors
1. White
2. Black
3. Graphite
4. Slate Grey
5. Graphite/Neutral Grey 1:1
6. Grey Sky
7. Light Cinnamon
8. Gingerbread
9. True Red
10. Cadmium Yellow

Eyes (detail)

Basset Hound

Palette
Black
White
Graphite
Neutral Grey
Grey Sky
Medium Flesh
Gingerbread
Light Cinnamon

Instructions
1. Trace drawing and transfer to paint surface.
2. Follow the diagram and paint areas as indicated.
3. Paint whisker dots Grey Sky.
4. Paint large areas of eye such as iris and pupil and add White highlights last.
5. Use Black and liner brush (or Black Ultra Fine Point Sharpie) to add outlining as shown in picture.

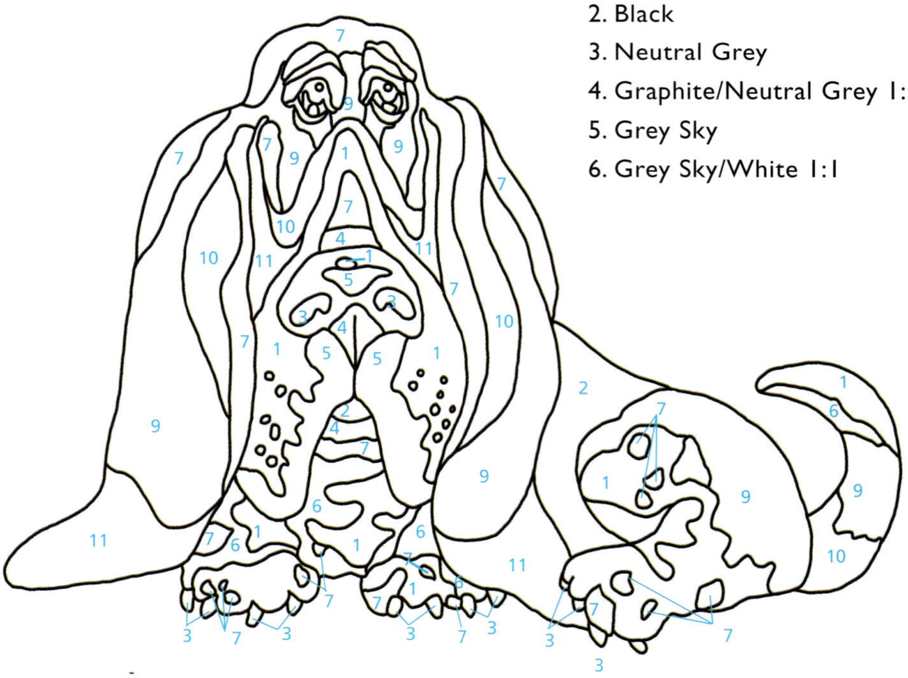

Colors
1. White
2. Black
3. Neutral Grey
4. Graphite/Neutral Grey 1:1
5. Grey Sky
6. Grey Sky/White 1:1
7. Medium Flesh
8. Medium Flesh/White 1:2
9. Gingerbread
10. Gingerbread/Light Cinnamon 1:1
11. Light Cinnamon

Eyes (detail)

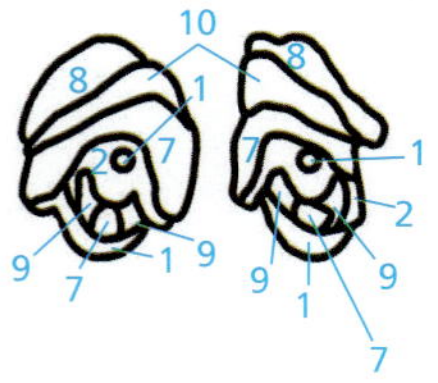

Birman

Palette

Black
White
Graphite
Neutral Grey
Grey Sky
Toffee
Medium Flesh
Gingerbread
Raspberry
Calypso

Instructions

1. Trace drawing and transfer to paint surface.
2. Follow the diagram and paint areas as indicated.
3. Paint large areas of eye such as iris and pupil and add White highlights last.
4. Use Neutral Grey and liner brush to add outlining as shown in picture.

Eyes (detail)

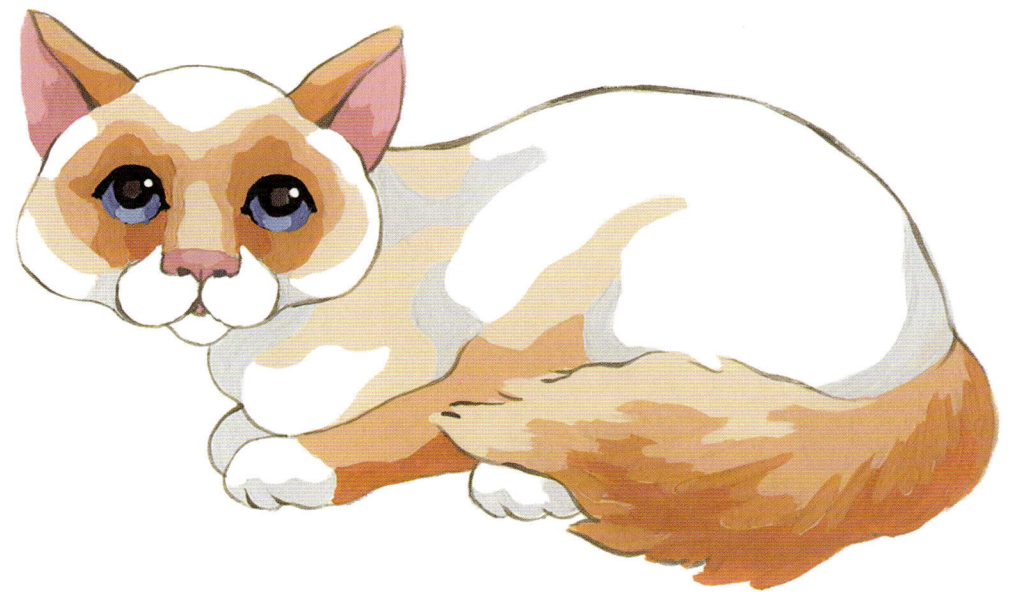

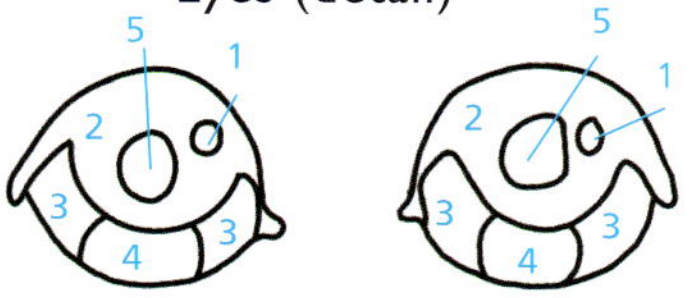

Nose/Mouth (detail)

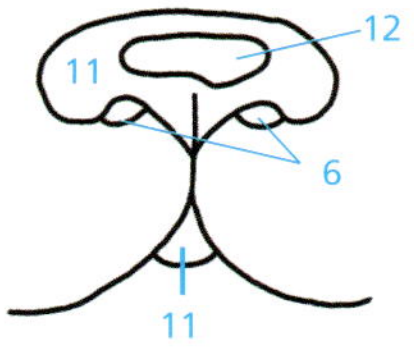

Colors

1. White
2. Black
3. Calypso
4. Calypso/White 1:1
5. Graphite/Neutral Grey 1:1
6. Neutral Grey
7. Medium Flesh
8. Medium Flesh/Gingerbread 1:1
9. Medium Flesh/White 1:1
10. Grey Sky/White 1:1
11. Raspberry/White 1:1
12. Raspberry/White 1:2
13. Toffee/White 1:1

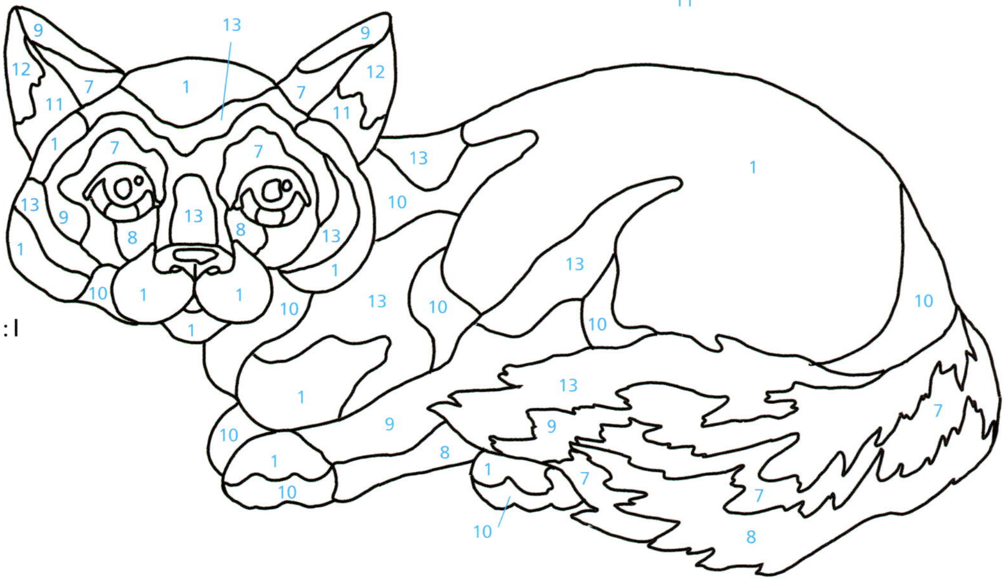

Don't Mess with Me!

Palette

Black
White
Graphite
Neutral Grey
Slate Grey
Grey Sky
Toffee
Honey Brown
Mississippi Mud
Baby Pink
Boysenberry Pink
Burnt Sienna
Burnt Orange

Instructions

1. Trace drawing and transfer to paint surface.
2. Follow the diagram and paint areas as indicated.
3. Paint toenails using Slate Grey.
4. Add highlights to nose using Light Grey mixture and White.
5. When painting eyes, fill in larger areas such as pupil and iris first and add White highlights over the top.
6. Paint eyes, nose, and mouth on skull using Black. Add teeth using White dots.
7. Add White dots for teeth on Bulldog.
8. Use Black Ultra Fine Point Sharpie to add outlining as shown in picture. Use Sharpie for lettering.

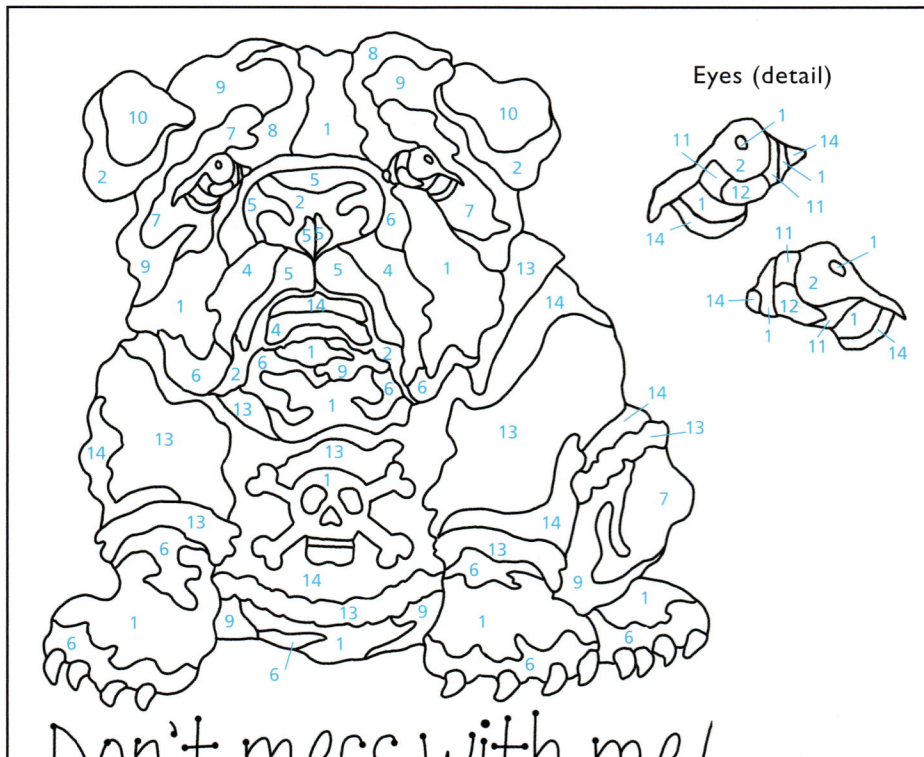

Eyes (detail)

Colors

1. White
2. Black
3. Neutral Grey
4. Slate Grey
5. Graphite/Neutral Grey 1:1
6. Grey Sky/White 1:1
7. Toffee
8. Honey Brown
9. Honey Brown/Toffee 2:1
10. Mississippi Mud
11. Burnt Sienna
12. Burnt Orange
13. Baby Pink
14. Baby Pink/Boysenberry Pink 1:1

My Red Bone

Palette
Black
White
Graphite
Neutral Grey
Honey Brown
Toffee
Light Cinnamon
Raspberry
True Red
Cherry Red
Cadmium Orange

Instructions
1. Trace drawing and transfer to paint surface.
2. Follow the diagram and paint areas as indicated.
3. Paint large areas of eye such as iris and pupil and add White highlights last.
4. Use liner brush and Black to add outlines to nose, eyes, mouth, and tongue.

Colors
1. White
2. Black
3. Graphite/Neutral Grey 1:1
4. Honey Brown
5. Honey Brown/Toffee 2:1
6. Honey Brown/Toffee 1:1
7. Toffee
8. Toffee/Honey Brown 2:1
9. Toffee/White 1:1
10. Toffee/White 1:2
11. Raspberry/White 1:1
12. Raspberry/White 1:2
13. Light Cinnamon
14. True Red
15. Cherry Red
16. Cadmium Orange

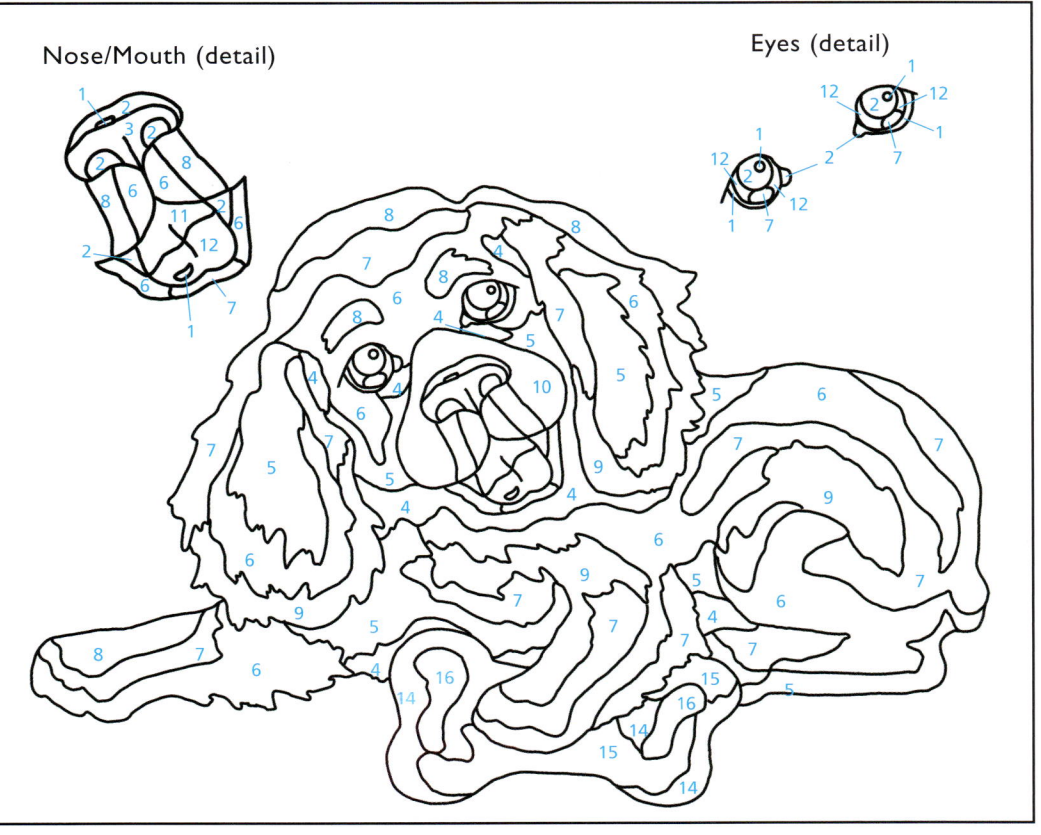

Pug

Palette
Black
White
Graphite
Neutral Grey
Toffee
Gingerbread
Raspberry
Mississippi Mud
Light Cinnamon

Instructions
1. Trace drawing and transfer to paint surface.
2. Follow the diagram and paint areas as indicated.
3. Paint large areas of eye such as iris and pupil and add White highlights last.

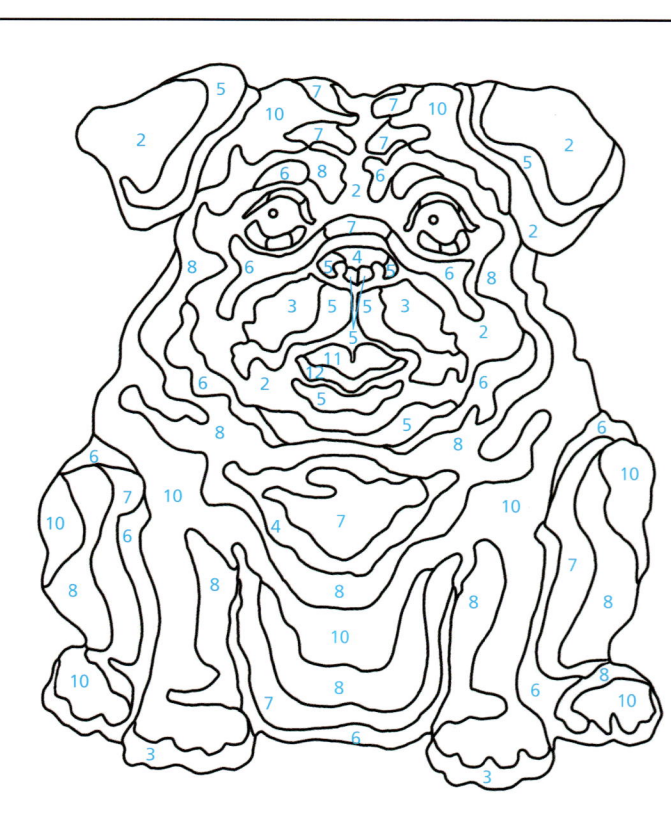

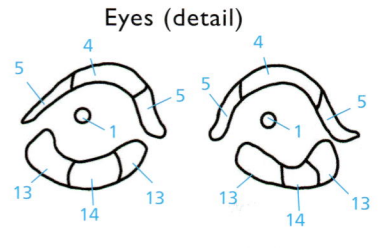

Eyes (detail)

Colors
1. White
2. Black
3. Graphite
4. Neutral Grey
5. Graphite/Neutral Grey 1:1
6. Mississippi Mud
7. Mississippi Mud/White 2:1
8. Mississippi Mud/White 1:1
9. Toffe/Mississippi Mud/White 2:1:1
10. Toffee/White 1:1
11. Raspberry
12. Raspberry/White 1:1
13. Light Cinnamon
14. Gingerbread

Schnauzer

Palette
Black
White
Grey Sky
Graphite
Neutral Grey
Slate Grey
Light Cinnamon
Gingerbread
Raspberry

Instructions
1. Trace drawing and transfer to paint surface.
2. Follow the diagram and paint areas as indicated.
3. Paint large areas of eye such as iris and pupil and add White highlights last.
4. Use Neutral Grey and liner brush to add outlining as shown in picture.

Colors
1. White
2. Black
3. Grey Sky
4. Slate
5. Graphite/Neutral Grey 1:1
6. Grey Sky/White 1:1
7. Light Cinnamon
8. Gingerbread
9. Raspberry/White 1:1

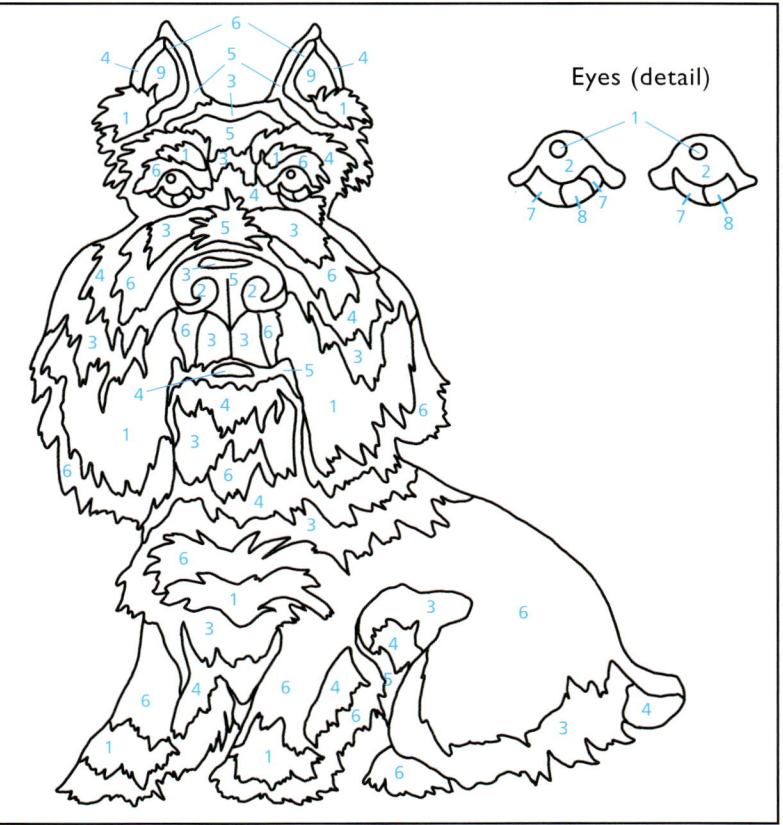

Best Buddy

Palette
Black
White
Graphite
Neutral Grey
Grey Sky
Slate Grey
Cadmium Yellow
Light Cinnamon
Gingerbread
Raspberry

Instructions
1. Trace drawing and transfer to paint surface.
2. Follow the diagram and paint areas as indicated.
3. Paint large areas of eye such as iris and pupil and add White highlights last.
4. Use Black Ultra Fine Point Sharpie or liner brush for outlining as shown in picture. Use a ruler and Black Sharpie for outlining on border.
5. Dip end of small brush in White and add dots on mouth for teeth.

Colors
1. White
2. Black
3. Light Cinnamon
4. Gingerbread
5. Graphite
6. Neutral Grey
7. Slate Grey
8. Grey Sky
9. Graphite/Neutral Grey 1:1
10. Grey Sky/White 1:1
11. Cadmium Yellow/White 1:1
12. Raspberry/White 1:1
13. Raspberry/White 1:2

Boxer

Palette
White
Black
Medium Flesh
Gingerbread
Cocoa
Cinnamon
Slate Grey
Grey Sky
Raspberry

Instructions
1. Trace drawing and transfer to paint surface.
2. Follow the diagram and paint areas as indicated.
3. Paint large areas of eye such as iris and pupil and add White highlights last.
4. Use Black Ultra Fine Point Sharpie to add outlining as shown in picture.

Colors
1. White
2. Black
3. Medium Flesh
4. Gingerbread
5. Cocoa/Gingerbread 1:2
6. Medium Flesh/Camel/White 1:1:1
7. Medium Flesh/Cinnamon 1:2
8. Slate Grey/Black 1:1
9. Grey Sky
10. Grey Sky/White 1:1
11. Raspberry/White 1:2

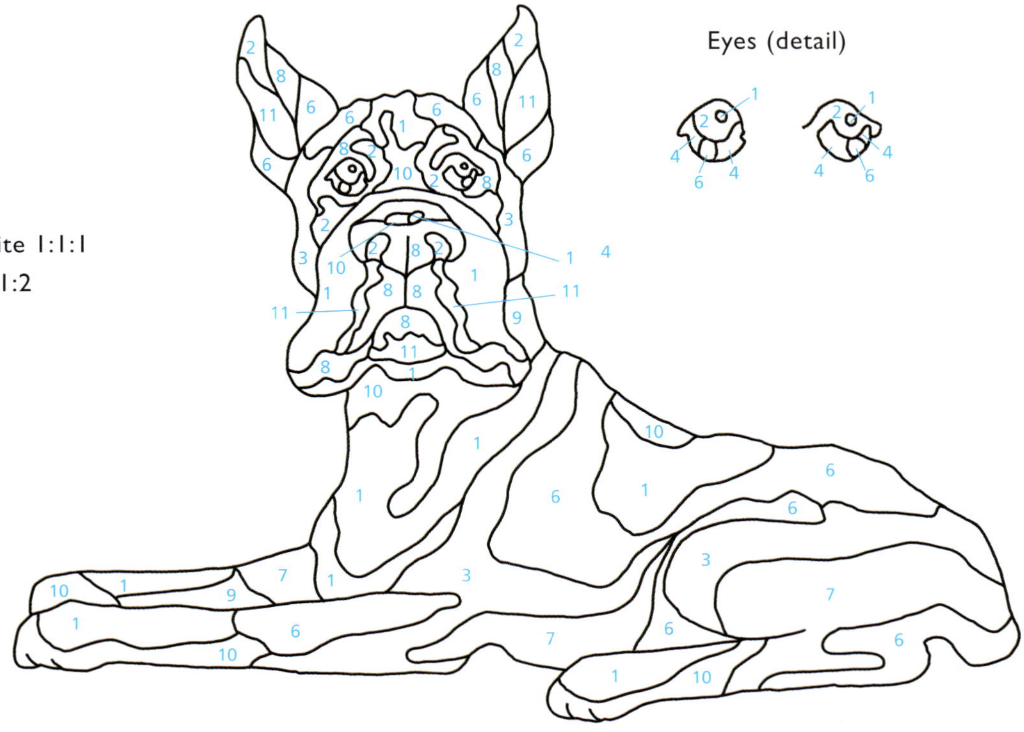

Eyes (detail)

Smile

Palette
White
Black
Raw Sienna
Camel
Slate Grey
Grey Sky
Gingerbread
Raspberry
Burnt Sienna

Instructions
1. Trace drawing and transfer to paint surface.
2. Follow the diagram and paint areas as indicated.
3. Paint large areas of eye such as iris and pupil and add White highlights last.
4. Use Black Ultra Fine Point Sharpie to add outlining as shown in picture.

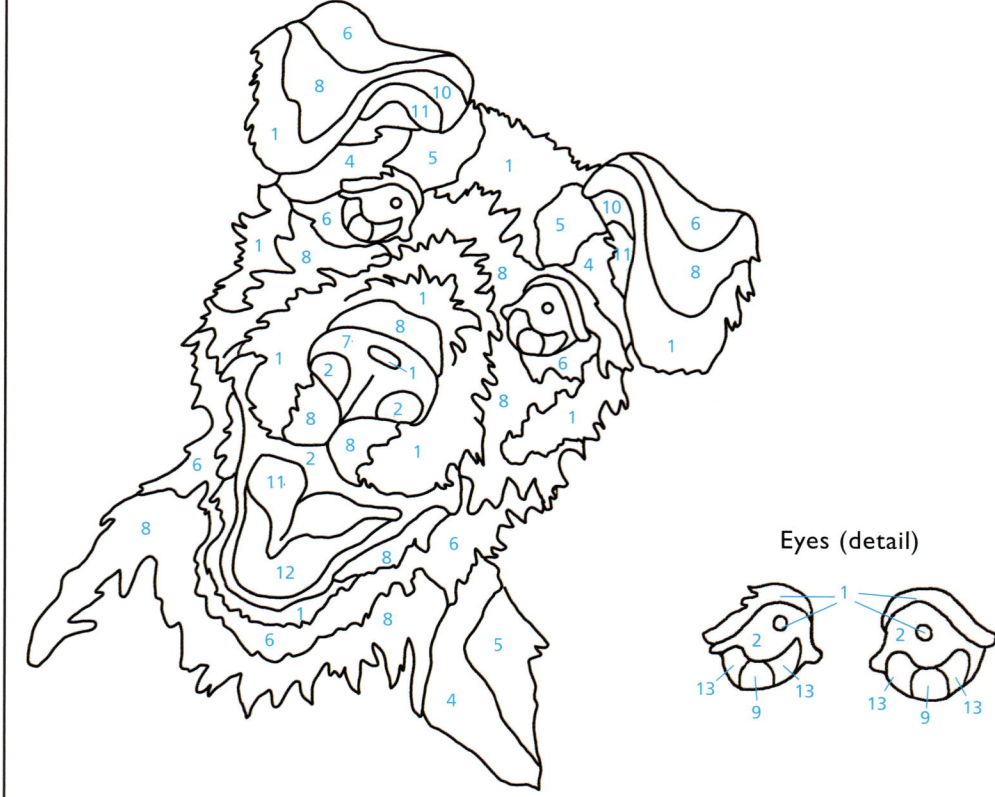

Eyes (detail)

Colors
1. White
2. Black
3. Raw Sienna
4. Raw Sienna/Camel 1:1
5. Raw Sienna/Camel 1:4
6. Slate Grey
7. Slate Grey/Black 1:1
8. Grey Sky/White 1:1
9. Gingerbread
10. Raspberry
11. Raspberry/White 1:1
12. Raspberry/White 1:3
13. Burnt Sienna

Chihuahua

Palette
White
Black
Grey Sky
Raw Sienna
Light Cinnamon
Gingerbread
Camel
Mocha
Raspberry

Instructions
1. Trace drawing and transfer to paint surface.
2. Follow the diagram and paint areas as indicated.
3. Paint large areas of eye such as iris and pupil and add White highlights last. Add dot of White to nose.
4. Use Black Ultra Fine Point Sharpie to add outlining as shown in picture.

Colors
1. White
2. Black
3. Grey Sky
4. Raw Sienna
5. Light Cinnamon
6. Gingerbread
7. Camel/Mocha/White 1:1:1
8. Camel/Mocha/White 1:1:4
9. Camel/Mocha 1:1
10. Grey Sky/White 1:1
11. Raspberry/White 1:1
12. Raspberry/White 1:2
13. Camel/Raw Sienna 1:2

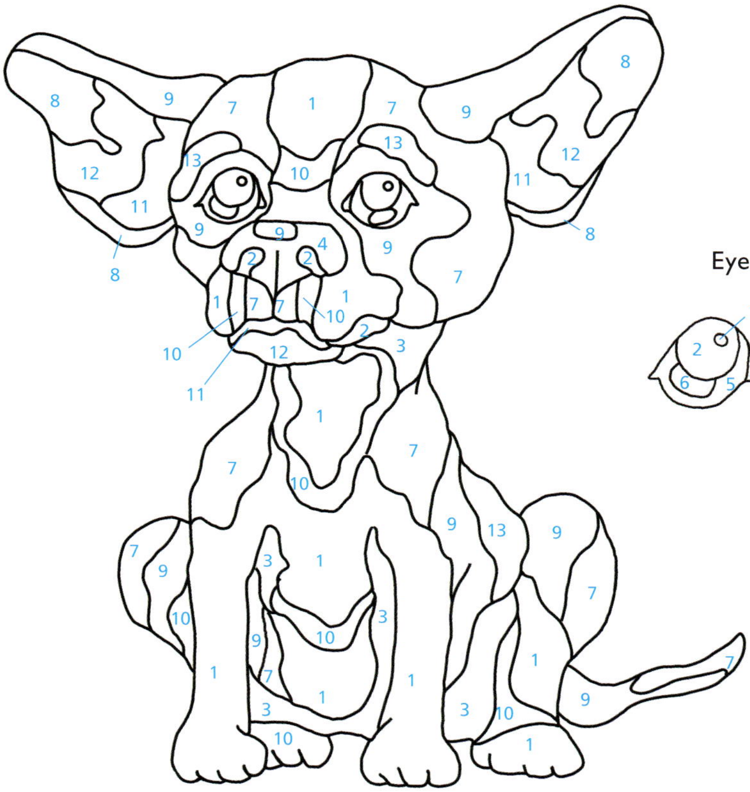

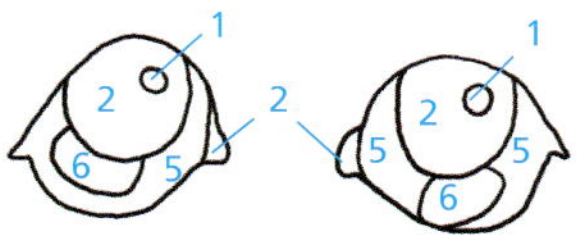

Everybody Needs a Teddy Bear

Palette

Black
White
Graphite
Neutral Grey
Grey Sky
Toffee
Light Cinnamon
Medium Flesh
Terra Cotta
Raspberry
Gingerbread

Instructions

1. Trace drawing and transfer to paint surface.
2. Follow the diagram and paint areas as indicated.
3. Paint freckles on muzzle Black.
4. Add tiny dot of White to Teddy Bear's eyes and highlight nose.
5. Paint large areas of eye such as iris and pupil and add White highlights last.
6. Use Black and liner brush to add outlining as shown in picture.

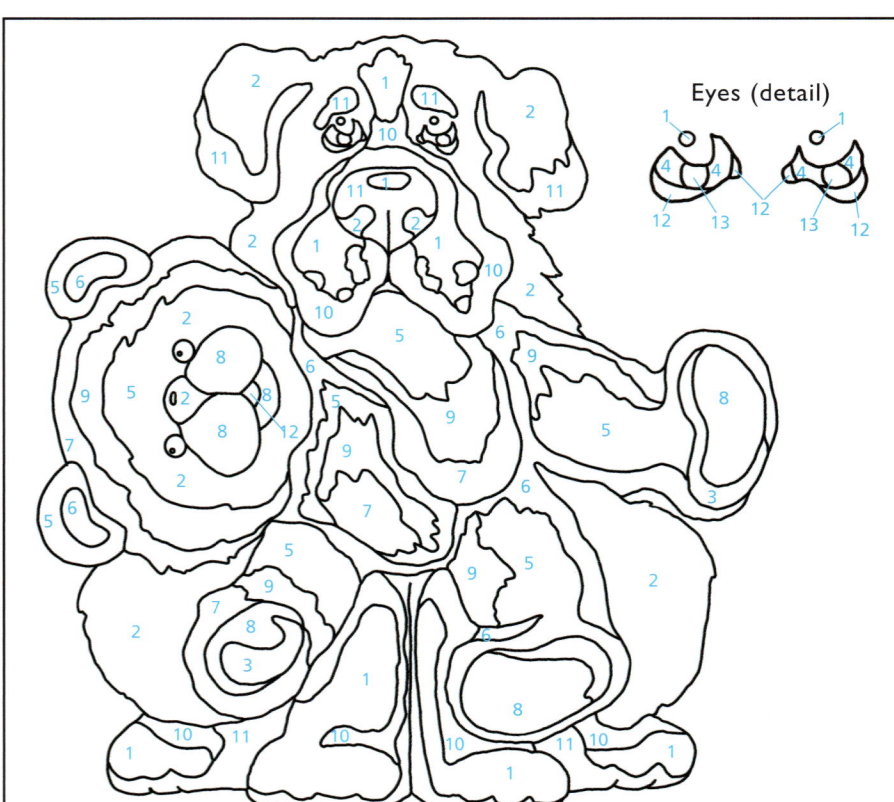

Eyes (detail)

Colors

1. White
2. Black
3. Toffee
4. Light Cinnamon
5. Medium Flesh
6. Terra Cotta/Medium Flesh 2:1
7. Medium Flesh/White 1:1
8. Toffee/White 1:1
9. Medium Flesh/White 2:1
10. Grey Sky/White 1:1
11. Graphite/Neutral Grey 1:1
12. Raspberry/White 1:1
13. Gingerbread

Golden Retriever

Palette

Black
White
Slate Grey
Cadmium Yellow
Gingerbread
Light Cinnamon
Camel
Mocha
Raw Sienna
Raspberry

Instructions

1. Trace drawing and transfer to paint surface.
2. Follow the diagram and paint areas as indicated.
3. Paint large areas of eye such as iris and pupil and add White highlights last.
4. Paint teeth White.
5. Add lines on yellow tennis ball using White and liner brush.
6. Add tiny dot of White to highlight nose.
7. Use Slate Grey and liner brush to add outlining as shown in picture.

Colors

1. White
2. Black
3. Slate Grey
4. Cadmium Yellow
5. Gingerbread
6. Light Cinnamon
7. Camel/Mocha 1:1
8. Camel/Mocha/White 1:1:1
9. Camel/Mocha/White 1:1:4
10. Camel/Raw Sienna 1:2
11. Black/Slate 1:1
12. Raspberry/White 1:1

Eyes (detail)

Dalmation

Palette
Black
White
Slate Grey
Grey Sky
Camel
Raspberry
Light Cinnamon
Gingerbread
True Red

Instructions
1. Trace drawing and transfer to paint surface.
2. Follow the diagram and paint areas as indicated.
3. Paint large areas of eye such as iris and pupil then add White highlight dot at upper left.
4. Dip end of brush in Camel and add three dots to collar.
5. Use Neutral Grey and liner brush to add outlining as shown in picture.

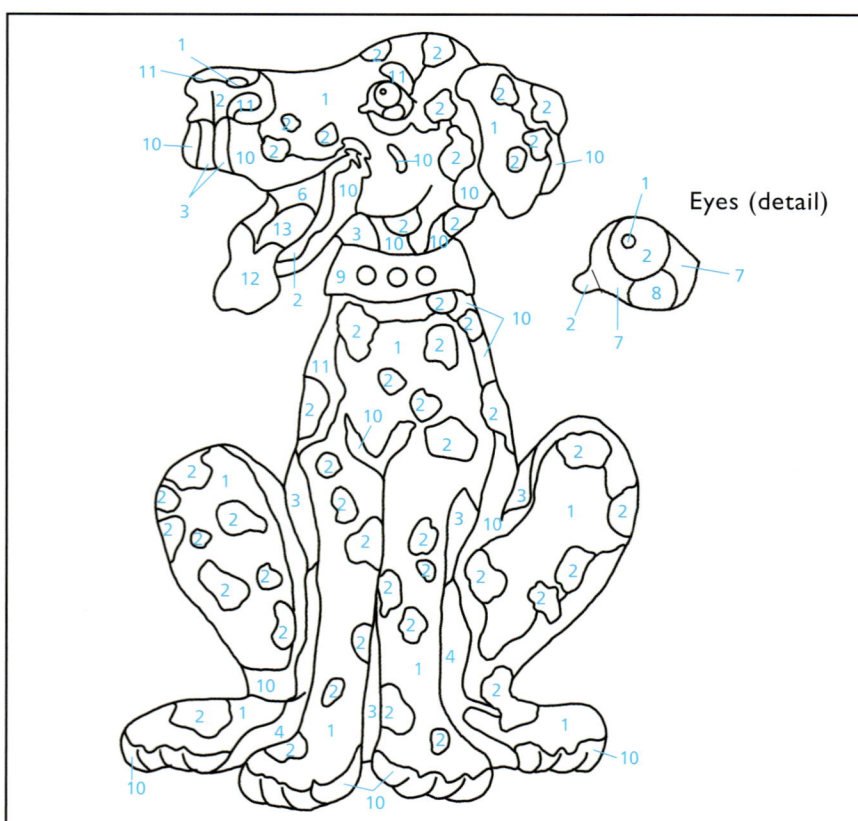

Colors
1. White
2. Black
3. Slate Grey
4. Grey Sky
5. Camel
6. Raspberry
7. Light Cinnamon
8. Gingerbread
9. True Red
10. Grey Sky/White 1:1
11. Slate Grey/Black 1:1
12. Raspberry/White 1:1
13. Raspberry/White 1:2

Welcome

Palette
Black
White
Moon Yellow
Dark Chocolate
Sable Brown
Baby Pink
Mocha
Honey Brown
Peony Pink
Slate Grey
Indian Turquoise
Olive Green

Instructions
1. Trace drawing and transfer to paint surface.
2. Follow the diagram and paint areas as indicated.
3. Paint eyes Black and add tiny dot of White for highlight.
4. Dip end of brush in #6 Baby Pink and add dots to large heart; paint small hearts #9 mix.
5. Use Black and liner brush to add outlining on dog as shown in picture.

Colors
1. White
2. Black
3. Moon Yellow
4. Dark Chocolate
5. Sable Brown
6. Baby Pink
7. Mocha
8. Honey Brown
9. Peony Pink/White 3:1
10. Mocha/White 1:1
11. Mocha/Honey Brown 1:1
12. Slate Grey/Black 1:1
13. Indian Turquoise
14. Slate Grey
15. Grey Sky/White 1:1
16. Olive Green/Moon Yellow 1:1

Pony

Palette
Black
White
Slate Grey
Grey Sky
Gingerbread
Medium Flesh
Light Cinnamon

Instructions
1. Trace drawing and transfer to paint surface.
2. Follow the diagram and paint areas as indicated.
3. Paint large areas of eye such as iris and pupil. Add White highlight dot at upper right.
4. Use Slate Grey and liner brush to add outlining as shown in picture.

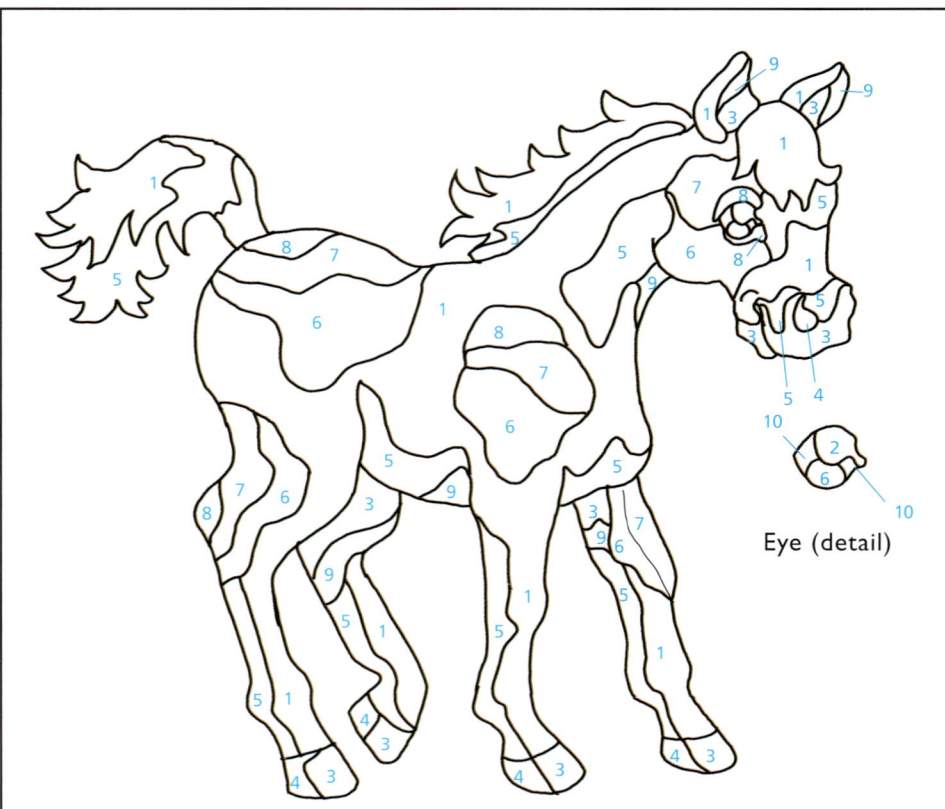

Eye (detail)

Colors
1. White
2. Black
3. Slate Grey
4. Slate/Black 1:1
5. Grey Sky/White 1:1
6. Gingerbread
7. Medium Flesh/Gingerbread 1:1
8. Medium Flesh/White 1:1
9. Grey Sky
10. Light Cinnamon

Box Fish

Palette
Black
Cadmium Yellow
Golden Straw
Taffy
Cadmium Red
Pumpkin

Instructions
1. Trace drawing and transfer to paint surface.
2. Follow the diagram and paint areas as indicated.
3. Paint spots on fish #1 Black.

Colors
1. Black
2. Cadmium Yellow
3. Golden Straw
4. Taffy
5. Cadmium Red/Pumpkin 1:1

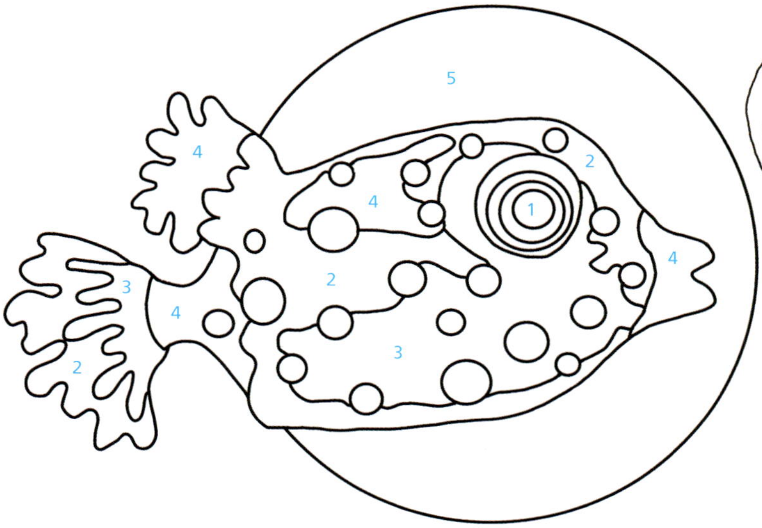

Eye (detail)

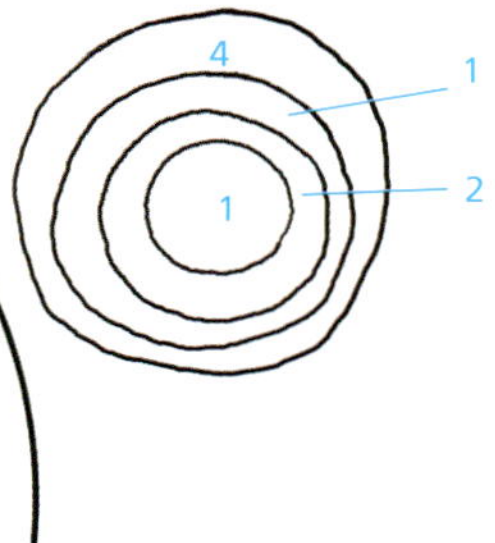

Goldfish

Palette
White
Black
Slate Grey
Marigold
Cadmium Yellow
Taffy
Raw Sienna

Instructions
1. Trace drawing and transfer to paint surface.
2. Follow the diagram and paint areas as indicated.
3. Paint scales #4 Marigold.
4. Dip end of small brush in #1 White and add dot to eye for highlight.

Colors
1. White
2. Black
3. Slate Grey
4. Marigold
5. Marigold/Cadmium Yellow 1:1
6. Cadmium Yellow/Taffy 1:1
7. Marigold/Raw Sienna 1:1
8. Cadmium Yellow/White 1:1
9. Cadmium Yellow

Trigger Fish

Palette
White
Black
Moon Yellow
Taffy
Marigold
Pumpkin
Blue Chiffon
Calypso Blue
Pumpkin
Cadmium Red

Instructions
1. Trace drawing and transfer to paint surface.
2. Follow the diagram and paint areas as indicated.
3. Dip end of small brush in #1 White and add dots to black fin and highlight in eye.
4. Use Black and liner brush or Black Ultra Fine Point Sharpie to add outlining as shown in picture.

Colors
1. White
2. Black
3. Moon Yellow
4. Taffy
5. Marigold
6. Pumpkin
7. Blue Chiffon
8. Calypso Blue
9. Pumpkin/White 1:1
10. Cadmium Red/Pumpkin 1:1
11. Calypso Blue/White 1:1

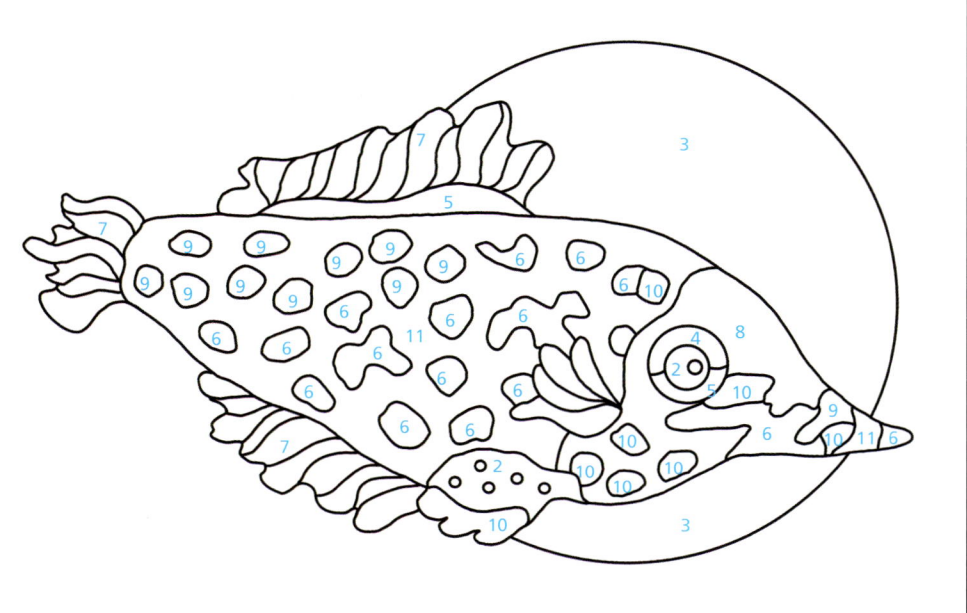

Kitty Face

Palette
Black
White
Mistletoe
Slate Grey
Olive Green
Grey Sky
Raspberry

Instructions
1. Trace drawing and transfer to paint surface.
2. Follow the diagram and paint areas as indicated.
3. Paint highlights in eyes using #1 White.
4. Use #4 Slate Grey and liner brush to paint whiskers.
5. Paint line from nose to mouth using #8 Raspberry mixture.
6. Paint mouth using #2 Black.

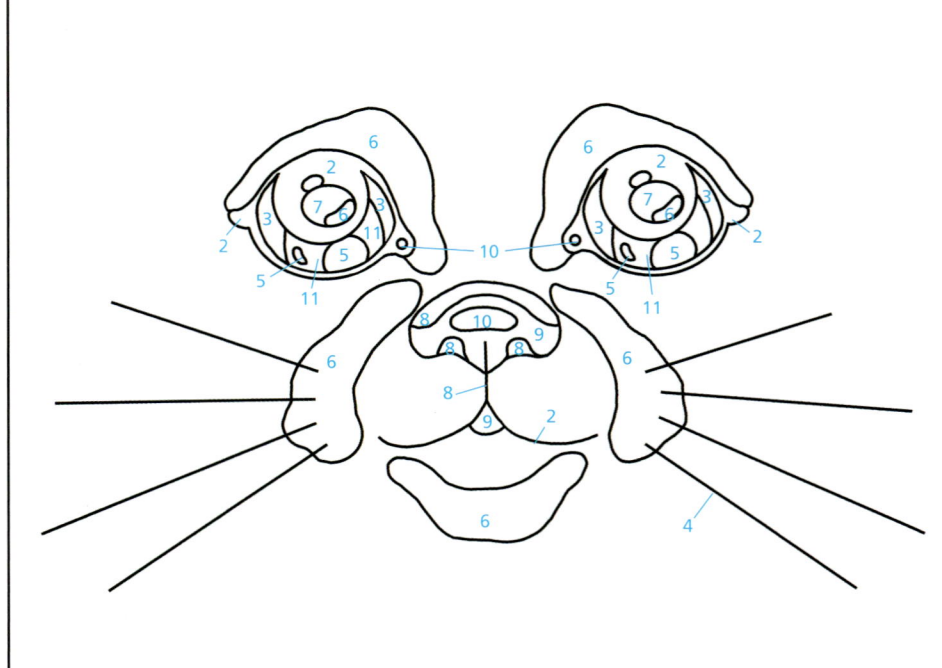

Colors
1. White
2. Black
3. Mistletoe
4. Slate Grey
5. Olive Green
6. Grey Sky/White 1:1
7. Slate/Black 1:1
8. Raspberry/White 1:1
9. Raspberry/White 1:2
10. Raspberry/White 1:3
11. Olive Green/Mistletoe 1:1

Siamese

Palette
Black
White
Dark Chocolate
True Ochre
Moon Yellow
Indian Turquoise
Sable
Mississippi Mud
Raw Umber
Antique White
Lavender

Instructions
1. Trace drawing and transfer to paint surface.
2. Follow the diagram and paint areas as indicated.
3. Paint large areas of eye such as iris and pupil and add White highlights last.
4. Dip end of small brush in #3 Dark Chocolate and add three dots on each side of muzzle.
5. Paint nostrils using #2 Black
6. Use Black and liner brush (or Black Sharpie) to add outlining as shown in picture.

Colors
1. White
2. Black
3. Dark Chocolate
4. True Ochre
5. Moon Yellow
6. Indian Turquoise
7. Sable/Mississippi Mud 1:1
8. Raw Umber/Mississippi Mud 1:1
9. Sable/Mississippi Mud/White 1:1:1
10. Antique White/White 1:1:5
11. Lavender/White 1:1
12. Lavender/White 1:2
13. Indian Turquoise/White 1:3

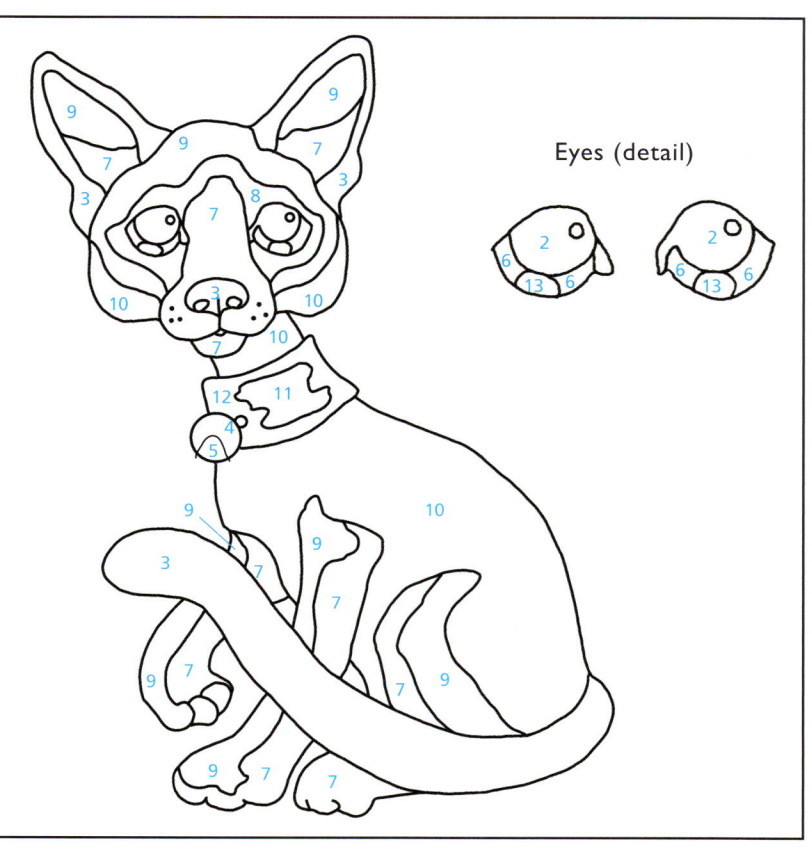

Bunny and Carrot

Palette
Black
White
Toffee
Honey Brown
Olive Green
Baby Pink
Raspberry
Canyon Orange
Pumpkin
Grey Sky
Hauser Light Green
Light Cinnamon

Instructions
1. Trace drawing and transfer to paint surface.
2. Follow the diagram and paint areas as indicated.
3. Paint large areas of eye such as iris and pupil and add White highlights last.
4. Use Black and liner brush for outlining as shown in picture.

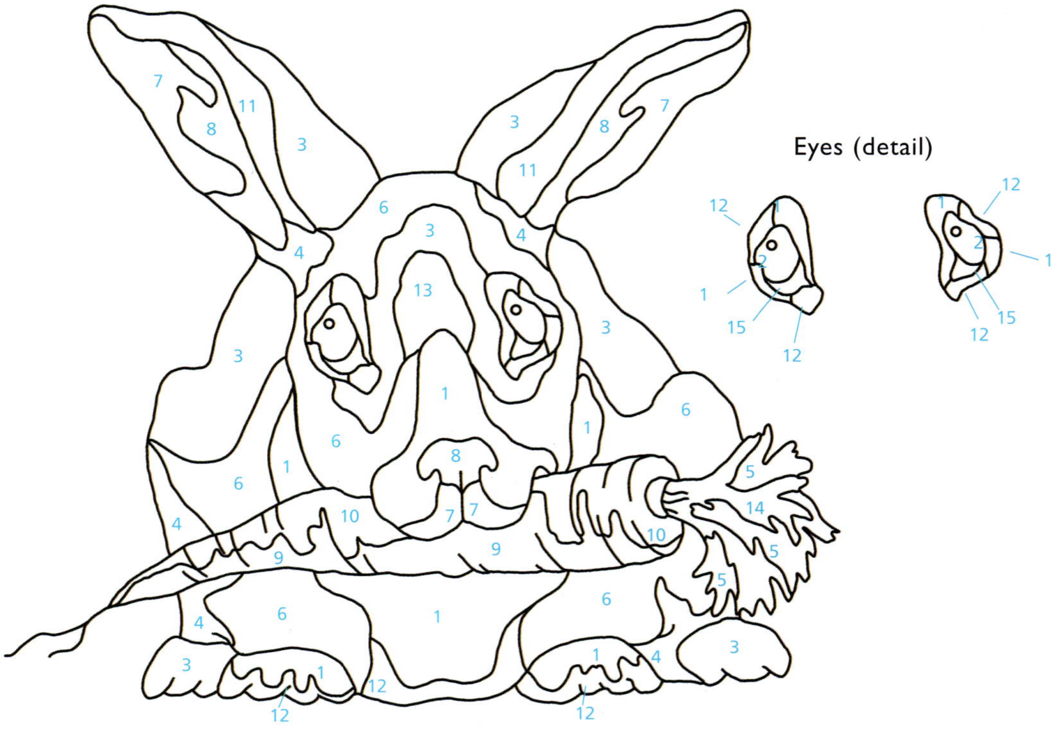

Colors
1. White
2. Black
3. Toffee
4. Honey Brown
5. Olive Green
6. Toffee/Honey Brown 1:1
7. Baby Pink/White 1:1
8. Raspberry/White 1:2
9. Canyon Orange/White 2:1
10. Pumpkin/White 1:1
11. Toffee/White 1:2
12. Grey Sky/White 1:1
13. Toffee/White 1:1
14. Hauser Light Green
15. Light Cinnamon

Black and White Bunny

Palette
Black
White
Slate Grey
Gingerbread
Light Cinnamon
Raspberry
Baby Pink
Grey Sky

Instructions
1. Trace drawing and transfer to paint surface.
2. Follow the diagram and paint areas as indicated.
3. Paint large areas of eye such as iris and pupil and add White highlights last.
4. Paint teeth #1 White.
5. Use #9 Black/Slate Grey mixture and liner brush for outlining as shown in picture.

Colors
1. White
2. Black
3. Slate Grey
4. Gingerbread
5. Light Cinnamon
6. Raspberry/White 1:1
7. Raspberry/White 1:2
8. Baby Pink/White 1:2
9. Black/Slate Grey 1:1
10. GreySky/White 1:1

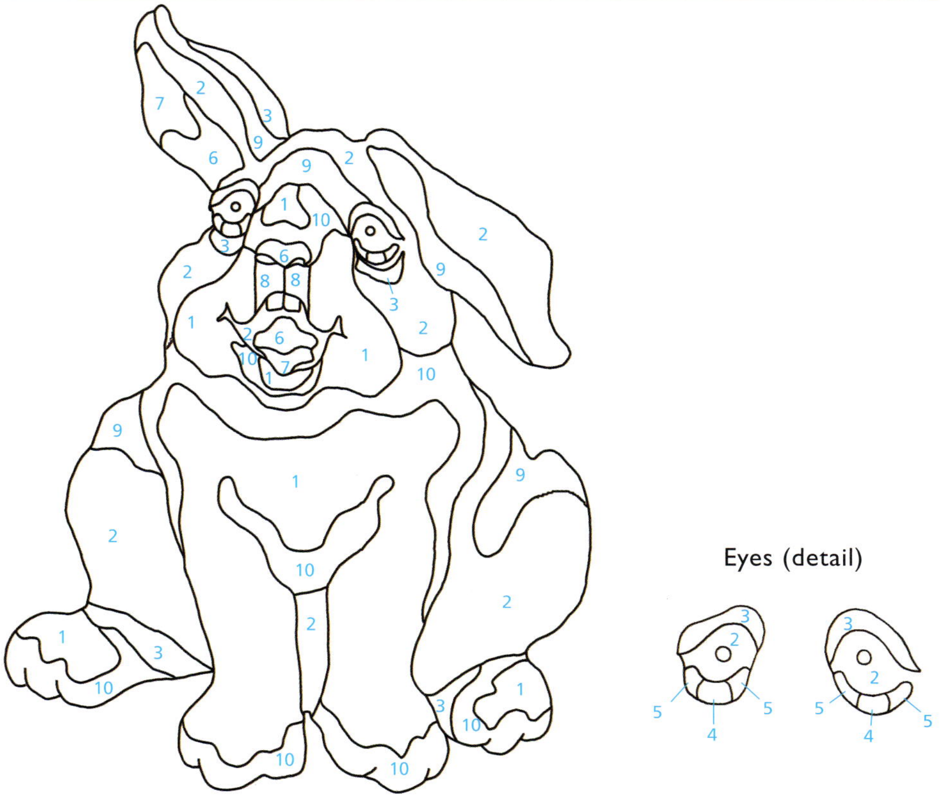

Eyes (detail)

Froggie

Palette
White
Black
Pumpkin
Cadmium Red
Cadmium Yellow
Petal Pink
Hauser Light Green
Jade
Yellow Green
Black Forest Green

Instructions
1. Trace drawing and transfer to paint surface.
2. Follow the diagram and paint areas as indicated.
3. Dip end of small brush in #1 White and add dot to eye for highlight.
4. Use Black and liner brush for nostrils.
5. Use Black Ultra Fine Point Sharpie to add outlining as shown in picture.

Colors
1. White
2. Black
3. Pumpkin
4. Cadmium Red
5. Cadmium Yellow
6. Petal Pink
7. Hauser Light Green
8. Hauser Light Green/Jade/Yellow Green 1:1:1
9. Black Forest Green

Cockatoo

Palette

Black
White
Lavender
Golden Straw
Olive Green
Slate Grey
True Red
Hauser Light Green
Grey Sky

Instructions

1. Trace drawing and transfer to paint surface.
2. Follow the diagram and paint areas as indicated.
3. Paint large areas of eye such as iris and pupil and add White highlight last.
4. Use Slate Grey and liner brush to add outlining as shown in picture.

Colors

1. White
2. Black
3. Lavender
4. Golden Straw
5. Olive Green
6. Slate Grey
7. True Red
8. Hauser Light Green
9. Grey Sky/White 1:1
10. Black/Slate Grey 1:1
11. Golden Straw/White 1:1
12. Grey Sky

Newfie Puppy

Palette
Black
White
Slate Grey
Cadmium Red
Deep Burgundy
Burnt Sienna
Cadmium Orange
Grey Sky
Raspberry

Instructions
1. Trace drawing and transfer to paint surface.
2. Follow the diagram and paint areas as indicated.
3. Paint large areas of eye such as iris and pupil and add White highlights last.
4. Paint freckles on muzzle #2 Black.
5. Use Black Ultra Fine Point Sharpie to add outlining as shown in picture.

Colors
1. White
2. Black
3. Slate Grey
4. Cadmium Red
5. Deep Burgundy
6. Burnt Sienna
7. Cadmium Orange/small amt. White
8. Slate Grey/Black 1:1
9. Grey Sky/White 1:1
10. Raspberry/White 1:1

Yorkie

Palette
Black
White
Medium Flesh
Mocha
Antique White
Gingerbread
Raw Sienna
Burnt Sienna
Buttermilk
Raspberry
Yellow Green
Bright Green
Hauser Dark Green
Slate Grey

Instructions
1. Trace drawing and transfer to paint surface.
2. Follow the diagram and paint areas as indicated.
3. Paint large areas of eye such as iris and pupil and add White highlights last.
4. Add dot of #1 White to nose for highlight.
5. Paint teeth #1 White.

Colors
1. White
2. Black
3. Hauser Dark Green
4. Bright Green
5. Yellow Green/Bright Green 1:1
6. Medium Flesh/White 1:1
7. Mocha/White 1:2
8. Antique White/White 1:3
9. Gingerbread/Raw Sienna 1:1
10. Medium Flesh
11. Medium Flesh/Gingerbread 1:2
12. Burnt Sienna
13. Raspberry/Buttermilk 1:1
14. Raspberry
15. Slate Grey/Black 1:1

Eyes (detail)

Poodle

Palette
Black
White
Slate Grey
Grey Sky
Raspberry
Burnt Sienna
Gingerbread

Instructions
1. Trace drawing and transfer to paint surface.
2. Follow the diagram and paint areas as indicated.
3. Paint large areas of eye such as iris and pupil and add White highlights last.
4. Use Black and liner brush (or Black Ultra Fine Point Sharpie) to add outlining as shown in picture.

Colors
1. White
2. Black
3. Slate Grey
4. Grey Sky
5. Grey Sky/White 1:1
6. Raspberry/White 1:2
7. Raspberry/White 3:1
8. Slate Grey/Black 1:1
9. Burnt Sienna
10. Gingerbread

Pomeranian

Palette

White
Black
Medium Flesh
Burnt Sienna
Gingerbread
Raspberry
Slate Grey
Grey Sky

Instructions

1. Trace drawing and transfer to paint surface.
2. Follow the diagram and paint areas as indicated.
3. Paint large areas of eye such as iris and pupil and add White highlights last.
4. Paint highlight on nose #12 Grey Sky mixture.

Colors

1. White
2. Black
3. Medium Flesh
4. Burnt Sienna
5. Gingerbread
6. Raspberry
7. Raspberry/White 1:1
8. Medium Flesh/White 1:1
9. Medium Flesh/White 1:3
10. Slate Grey/Black 1:1
11. Medium Flesh/Gingerbread 1:1
12. Grey Sky/White 1:1

Eyes (detail)

Walk???

Palette
Black
White
Cadmium Red
Burnt Sienna
Grey Sky
Slate Grey
Mocha
Cinnamon
Deep Burgundy
Raspberry

Instructions
1. Trace drawing and transfer to paint surface.
2. Follow the diagram and paint areas as indicated.
3. Paint large areas of eye such as iris and pupil and add highlights last.
4. Use Black and liner brush (or Black Ultra Fine Point Sharpie) to paint lettering and outlines an shown in picture.

Colors
1. White
2. Black
3. Grey Sky
4. Cadmium Red
5. Burnt Sienna
6. Grey Sky/White 1:1
7. Slate Grey/Black 1:1
8. Raspberry/White 1:1
9. Mocha/Cinnamon 2:1
10. Mocha/Cinnamon 1:4
11. Mocha/White 1:1
12. Deep Burgundy

Dogs Have Owners, Cats Have Staff

Palette
White
Black
Arbor Green
Primary Yellow
Raspberry
French Grey Blue
Grey Sky

Instructions
1. Trace drawing and transfer to paint surface.
2. Follow the diagram and paint areas as indicated.
3. Paint large areas of eye such as iris and pupil and add White highlights last.
4. Use Black Ultra Fine Point Sharpie or Black paint and liner brush to add outlining as shown in picture.

Colors
1. White
2. Black
3. Arbor Green
4. Primary Yellow
5. Raspberry
6. French Grey Blue/Grey Sky 1:1
7. French Grey Blue/Grey Sky/White 1:1:2
8. Grey Sky/White 1:1
9. Raspberry/White 1:2

Puppy Love

Palette

Black
White
Cocoa
Light Cinnamon
Gingerbread
Medium Flesh
Mocha
Cinnamon

Slate Grey
Cadmium Yellow
Sapphire
Raspberry
Cadmium Red
Grey Sky
Mississippi Mud

Instructions

1. Trace drawing and transfer to paint surface.
2. Follow the diagram and paint areas as indicated.
3. Paint large areas of eye such as iris and pupil and add White highlights on noses last.
4. Use Black and liner brush (or Black Ultra Fine Point Sharpie) to add outlining as shown in picture.
5. Paint lettering #12 Sapphire.

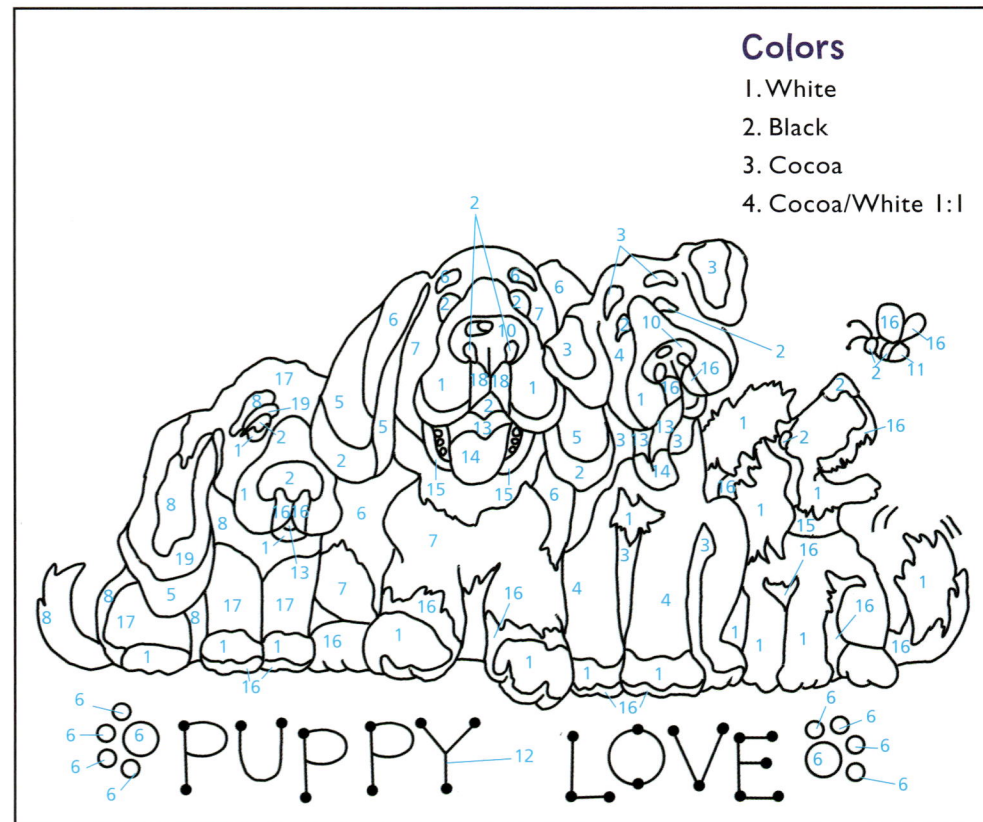

Colors

1. White
2. Black
3. Cocoa
4. Cocoa/White 1:1
5. Light Cinnamon
6. Gingerbread
7. Gingerbread/Medium Flesh 1:1
8. Mocha
9. Medium Flesh/Cinnamon 2:1
10. Slate Grey/Black 1:1
11. Cadmium Yellow
12. Sapphire
13. Raspberry/White 1:2
14. Raspberry/White 1:3
15. Cadmium Red
16. Grey Sky/White 1:1
17. Mocha/White 1:2
18. Slate Grey
19. Mississippi Mud

Relax

Palette

Black
White
Indian Turquoise
Grey Sky
Sable
Mississippi Mud
Raw Umber
Raspberry

Instructions

1. Trace drawing and transfer to paint surface.
2. Follow the diagram and paint areas as indicated.
3. Paint large areas of eye such as iris and pupil and add White highlights last.
4. Use Black Ultra Fine Point Sharpie for outlining as shown in picture.
5. Paint lettering #11 mix and dots between letters #14 Raw Umber.

Colors

1. White
2. Black
3. Indian Turquoise
4. Grey Sky
5. Indian Turquoise/White 1:1
6. Indian Turquoise/White 1:4
7. White/Grey Sky/Indian Turquoise 2:1:5
8. Sable/Mississippi Mud 1:1
9. Sable/Mississippi Mud/White 1:1:1
10. Sable/Mississippi Mud/White 1:1:2
11. Raw Umber/Mississippi 1:1
12. Raspberry/White 1:1
13. Raspberry
14. Raw Umber
15. Grey Sky/White 1:2

Eyes (detail)

Jack Russell Terrier

Palette
Black
White
Slate Grey
Grey Sky
Medium Flesh
Gingerbread
Cocoa
Raspberry

Instructions
1. Trace drawing and transfer to paint surface.
2. Follow the diagram and paint areas as indicated.
3. Paint large areas of eye such as iris and pupil and add White highlights last.
4. Use Slate Grey/Black #8 mixture and liner brush to add outlining as shown in picture.

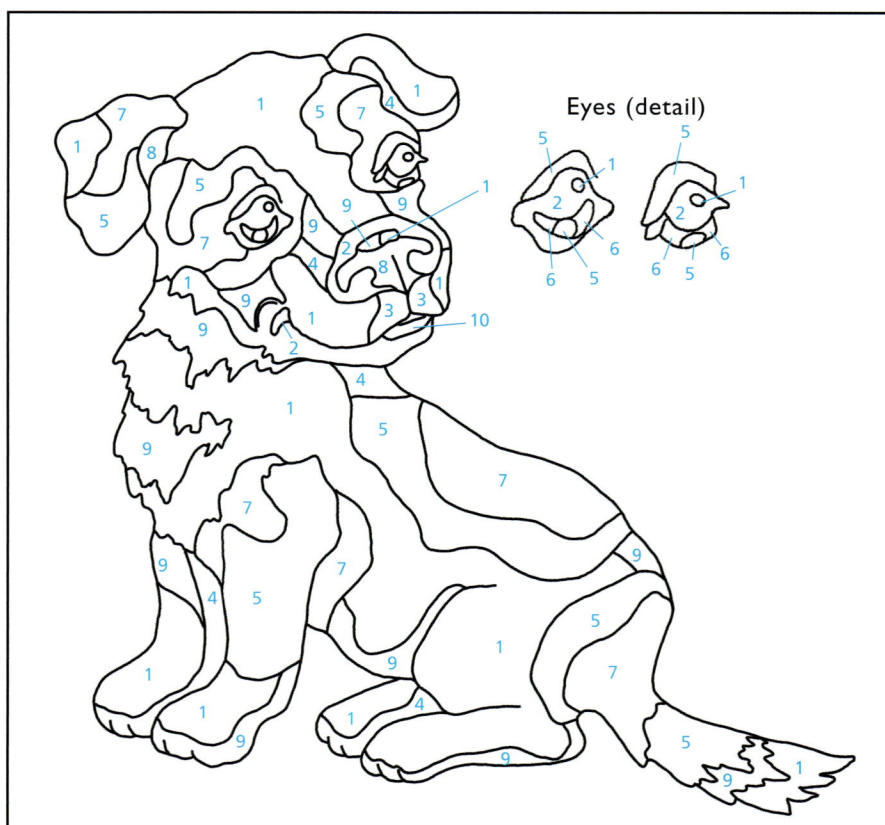

Eyes (detail)

Colors
1. White
2. Black
3. Slate Grey
4. Grey Sky
5. Medium Flesh
6. Gingerbread
7. Cocoa/Gingerbread 1:1
8. Slate Grey/Black 1:1
9. Grey Sky/White 1:1
10. Raspberry/White 1:2

Purple Bunny

Palette

Black
White
Cadmium Red
Lavender
Dark Chocolate
Antique White
Gingerbread
Medium Flesh
Raw Sienna

Instructions

1. Trace drawing and transfer to paint surface.
2. Follow the diagram and paint areas as indicated.
3. Paint large areas of eye such as iris and pupil and add highlights last.
4. Use Black Ultra Fine Point Sharpie to add outlining as shown in picture.

Colors

1. White
2. Black
3. Cadmium Red
4. Lavender
5. Dark Chocolate
6. Antique White/White 1:1
7. Gingerbread
8. Gingerbread/Medium Flesh 2:1
9. Medium Flesh/White 2:1
10. Medium Flesh/White 1:2
11. Raw Sienna/Gingerbread 1:2

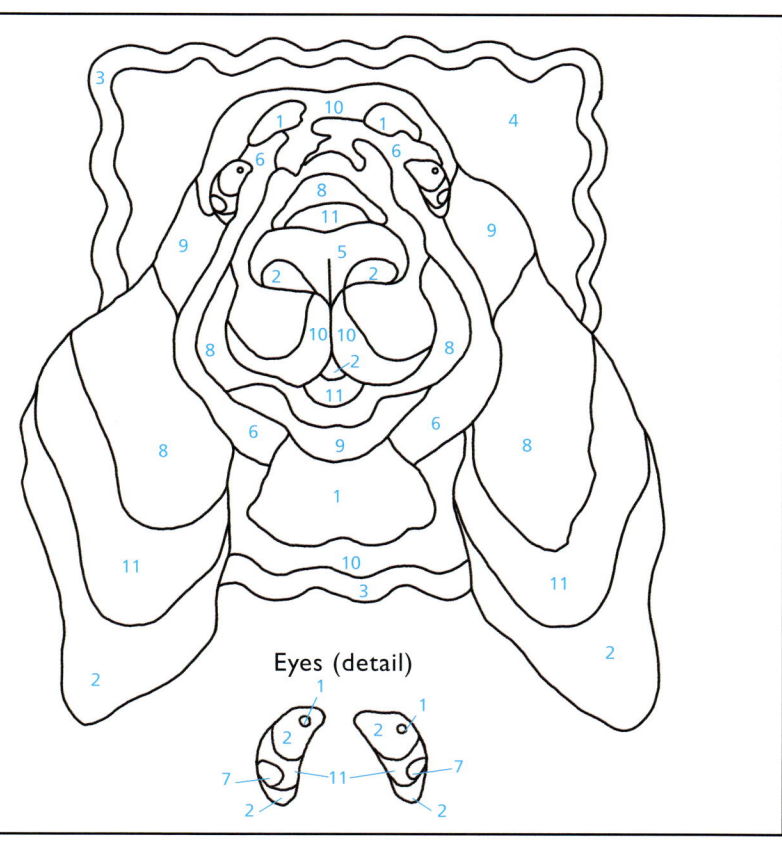

Eyes (detail)

Orange Kitty

Palette
Black
White
Calypso Blue
Pumpkin
Gingerbread
Medium Flesh
Grey Sky
Raspberry

Instructions
1. Trace drawing and transfer to paint surface.
2. Follow the diagram and paint areas as indicated.
3. Paint large areas of eye such as iris and pupil and add White highlights last.
4. Use Black Ultra Fine Point Sharpie to add outlining as shown in picture.

Colors
1. White
2. Black
3. Calypso Blue
4. Pumpkin/Gingerbread 1:1
5. Pumpkin/Medium Flesh 1:1
6. Medium Flesh/White 1:2
7. Grey Sky/White 1:1
8. Raspberry/White 2:1
9. Raspberry/White 1:2

Dachshund

Palette

White, Camel
Black, Medium Flesh
Slate Grey, Buttermilk
Burnt Sienna, Grey Sky
Raw Sienna, Dark Chocolate

Instructions

1. Trace drawing and transfer to paint surface.
2. Follow the diagram and paint areas as indicated.
3. Paint large areas of eyes such as iris and pupil and add White highlights last.
4. Paint small area on nose #10 Grey Sky; add #1 White dot for highlight.
5. Use Black and liner brush (or Black Ultra Fine Point Sharpie) to add outlining as shown in picture.

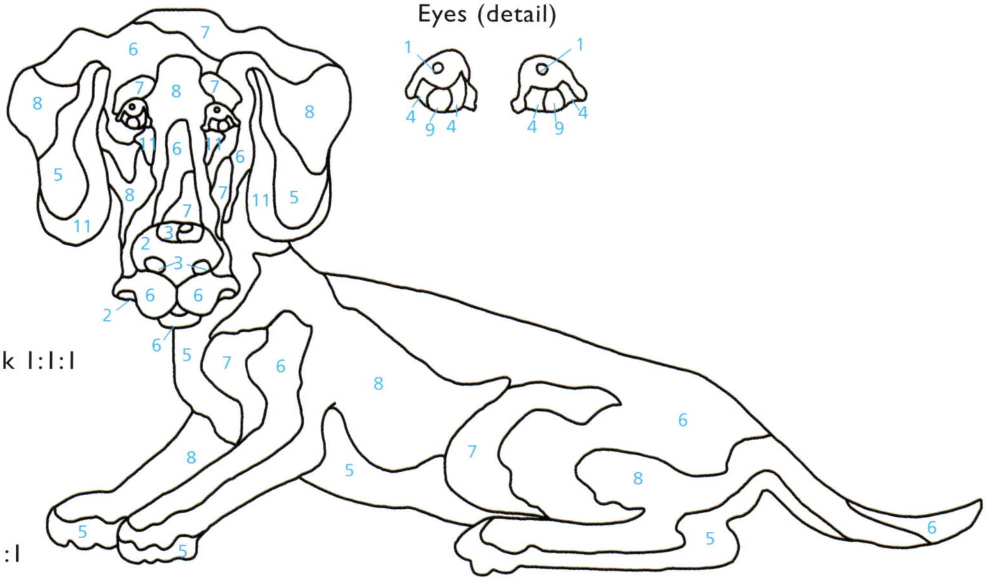

Colors

1. White
2. Black
3. Slate Grey/Black 1:1
4. Burnt Sienna
5. Raw Sienna
6. Camel/Medium Flesh/Buttermilk 1:1:1
7. Antique White/Buttermilk 1:1
8. Raw Sienna/Camel 3:1
9. Burnt Sienna/Medium Flesh
10. Grey Sky
11. Dark Chocolate/Raw Sienna 1:1

Eyes (detail)

Cat People

Palette
Black
White
Graphite
Blush Flesh
Cadmium Yellow
True Ochre
Sapphire
Grey Sky
Yellow Green

Instructions
1. Trace drawing and transfer to paint surface.
2. Follow the diagram and paint areas as indicated.
3. Paint large areas of eye such as iris and pupil and add White highlights last.
4. Paint nostril #2 Black.
5. Use Black Ultra Fine Point Sharpie to add outlining and lettering as shown in picture.

Eyes (detail)

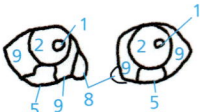

Colors
1. White
2. Black
3. Graphite
4. Blush Flesh
5. Cadmium Yellow/White/True Ochre 3:1:1
6. Sapphire/White 3:1
7. Grey Sky/White 1:1
8. Blush Flesh/White 1:1
9. Yellow Green
10. Grey Sky

Cocker Spaniel

Palette

Black
White
Slate Grey
Camel
Medium Flesh
Raw Sienna
Raspberry
Gingerbread
Grey Sky

Instructions

1. Trace drawing and transfer to paint surface.
2. Follow the diagram and paint areas as indicated.
3. Paint large areas of eye such as iris and pupil and add White highlights last.
4. Add dot of #1 White to nose for highlight; paint teeth #1 White.
5. Use Black Ultra Fine Point Sharpie to add outlines on face as shown in picture.

Colors

1. White
2. Black
3. Slate Grey/Black 1:1
4. Camel/Medium Flesh 1:1
5. Raw Sienna/small amt. of Camel
6. Camel/White 1:1
7. Camel/White 1:2
8. Raspberry/White 2:1
9. Raspberry/White 1:2
10. Gingerbread
11. Grey Sky

German Shepherd

Palette
White
Black
Raw Sienna
Slate Grey
Camel
Medium Flesh
Buttermilk
Antique White
Raspberry
Grey Sky

Instructions
1. Trace drawing and transfer to paint surface.
2. Follow the diagram and paint areas as indicated.
3. Paint large areas of eye such as iris and pupil and add White highlights last.
4. Add dot of #1 White to nose for highlight.
5. Paint teeth #1 White.

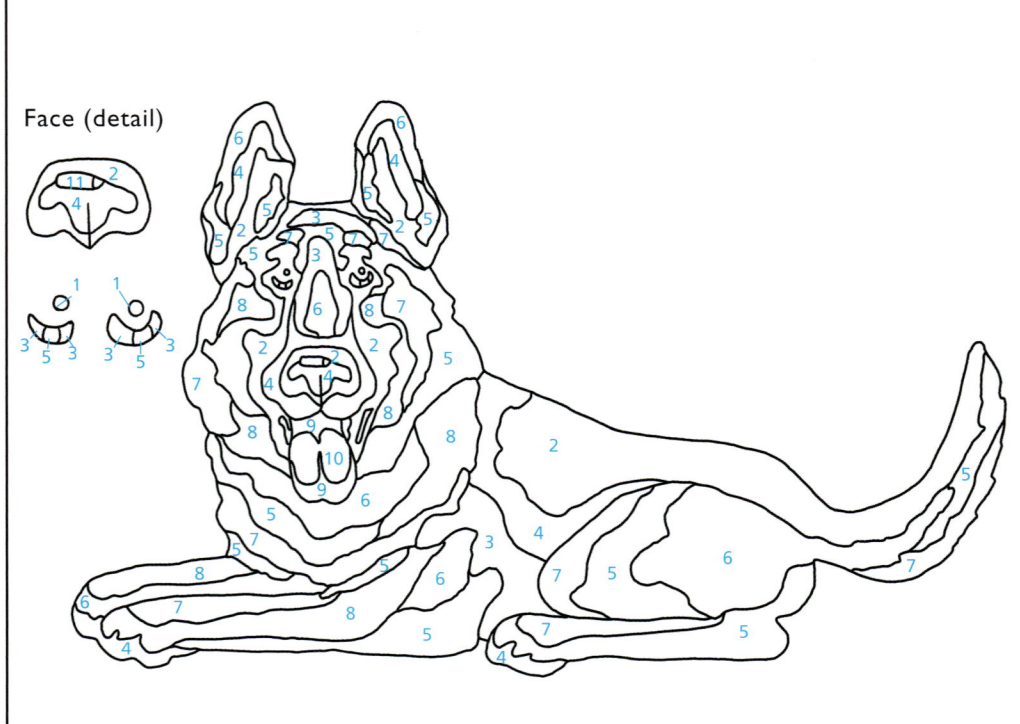

Colors
1. White
2. Black
3. Raw Sienna
4. Black/Slate Grey 1:1
5. Camel/Medium Flesh/Buttermilk 1:1:1
6. Raw Sienna/Camel 1:1
7. Antique White/Buttermilk 1:1
8. Antique White
9. Raspberry/White 1:1
10. Raspberry/White 1:2
11. Grey Sky/White 1:1

Himalayan

Palette

Black
White
French Grey Blue
Raspberry
Sapphire

Instructions

1. Trace drawing and transfer to paint surface.
2. Follow the diagram and paint areas as indicated.
3. Paint large areas of eye such as iris and pupil and add White highlights last.
4. Add three tiny dots to each side of muzzle using #4 mixture.
5. Use Black Ultra Fine Point Sharpie to add outlining as shown in picture.

Colors

1. White
2. Black
3. French Grey Blue
4. French Grey Blue/White 1:1
5. French Grey Blue/White 1:2
6. French Grey Blue/White 1:5
7. Raspberry/White 1:1
8. Sapphire
9. Sapphire/White 1:2

Face (detail)

Rottweiler

Palette
White
Black
Burnt Sienna
Slate Grey
Grey Sky
Raspberry
Gingerbread
Mocha

Instructions
1. Trace drawing and transfer to paint surface.
2. Follow the diagram and paint areas as indicated.
3. Paint large areas of eye such as iris and pupil and add White highlights last.
4. Paint teeth #1 White.
5. Use Black Ultra Fine Point Sharpie or Black paint and liner brush to add line on nose as shown in picture.

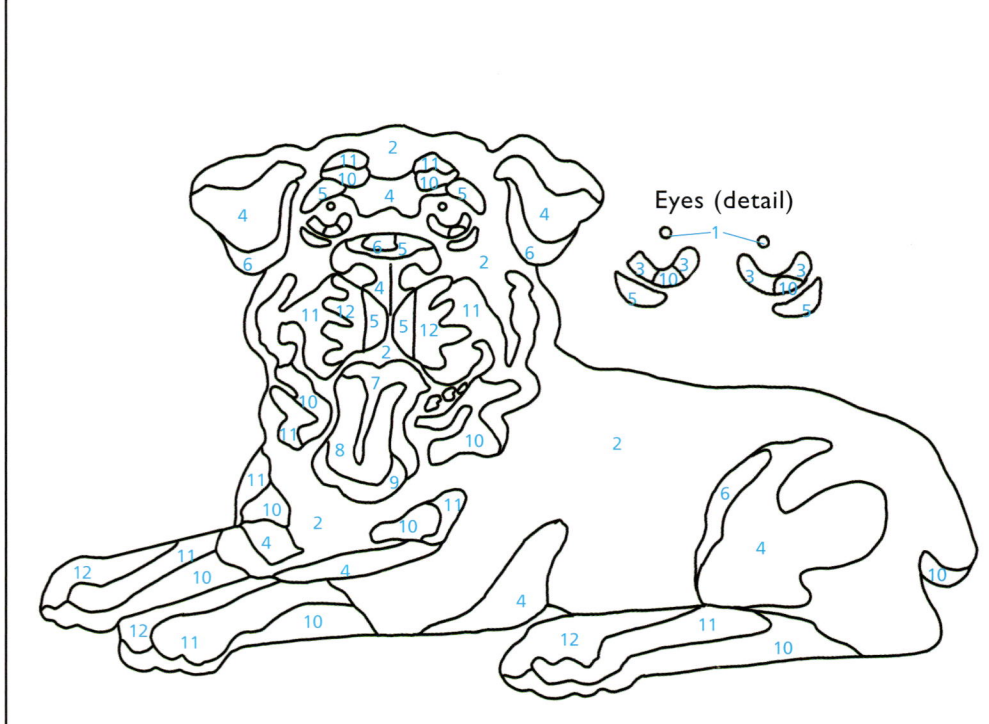

Eyes (detail)

Colors
1. White
2. Black
3. Burnt Sienna
4. Black/Slate Grey 1:1
5. Grey Sky
6. Grey Sky/White 1:1
7. Raspberry
8. Raspberry/White 1:1
9. Raspberry/White 1:2
10. Gingerbread
11. Gingerbread/Mocha 1:1
12. Mocha

Love a Bunny

Palette
White
Black
Slate Grey
Calypso Blue
Raspberry
Baby Pink
Mississippi Mud
Grey Sky

Instructions
1. Trace drawing and transfer to paint surface.
2. Follow the diagram and paint areas as indicated.
3. Paint large areas of eye such as iris and pupil and add White highlight last.
4. Use Black Ultra Fine Point Sharpie to add outlining as shown in picture.

Colors
1. White
2. Black
3. Slate Grey
4. Grey Sky/White 1:1
5. Calypso Blue/White 1:1
6. Raspberry/White 1:2
7. Baby Pink/White 1:2
8. Mississippi Mud
9. Grey Sky

Eyes (detail)

Love Birds

Palette
White
Black
Slate Grey
Grey Sky
Cadmium Red
Pumpkin
French Vanilla
Peaches 'n Cream
Bright Green
Evergreen
Hauser Light Green
Olive Green
Deep Burgundy
Raw Sienna

Instructions
1. Trace drawing and transfer to paint surface.
2. Follow the diagram and paint areas as indicated.
3. Paint large areas of eye such as iris and pupil and add White highlights last.
4. Paint feet #4 Grey Sky; paint toenails #2 Black.
5. Use Black Ultra Fine Point Sharpie or Black paint and liner brush to add outlining as shown in picture.

Colors
1. White
2. Black
3. Slate Grey
4. Grey Sky
5. Cadmium Red
6. Pumpkin
7. French Vanilla
8. Peaches 'n Cream
9. Bright Green
10. Bright Green/Evergreen 1:1
11. Hauser Lt. Green/Olive Green 1:1
12. Peaches 'n Cream/Pumpkin 1:1
13. Cadmium Red/Pumpkin 1:1
14. Cadmium Red/Deep Burgundy 1:1
15. Raw Sienna
16. Raw Sienna/White 1:1

Turtle

Palette
Black
White
Teal Green
Salem Blue
Gingerbread
French Grey Blue
Buttermilk
Pistachio Mint
Green Mist
Medium Flesh
Sapphire

Instructions
1. Trace drawing and transfer to paint surface.
2. Follow the diagram and paint areas as indicated.
3. Paint large areas of eye such as iris and pupil and add White highlight last.
4. Use Black Ultra Fine Point Sharpie to add outlining as shown in picture.

Colors
1. White
2. Black
3. Teal Green
4. Salem Blue
5. Gingerbread
6. French Grey Blue
7. Buttermilk
8. Pistachio Mint/Green Mist 2:1
9. Medium Flesh
10. Salem/White 1:4
11. Medium Flesh/White 1:2
12. Salem Blue/Teal Green 1:1
13. Pistachio/Green Mist/White 1:1:1
14. Salem Blue/Sapphire/White 2:1:1

Three Kitties

Palette
White
Black
Shading Flesh
Raw Umber
Yellow Green
Grey Sky
Slate Grey
Calypso Blue
Granite
Camel
Raspberry
Light Cinnamon
Antique White

Instructions
1. Trace drawing and transfer to paint surface.
2. Follow the diagram and paint areas as indicated.
3. Paint large areas of eye such as iris and pupil and add White highlights last.
4. Use Slate Grey paint and liner brush to add outlining as shown in picture.
5. Add three tiny Slate Grey dots to muzzle of top kitty.
6. Add Black dots for nostrils.

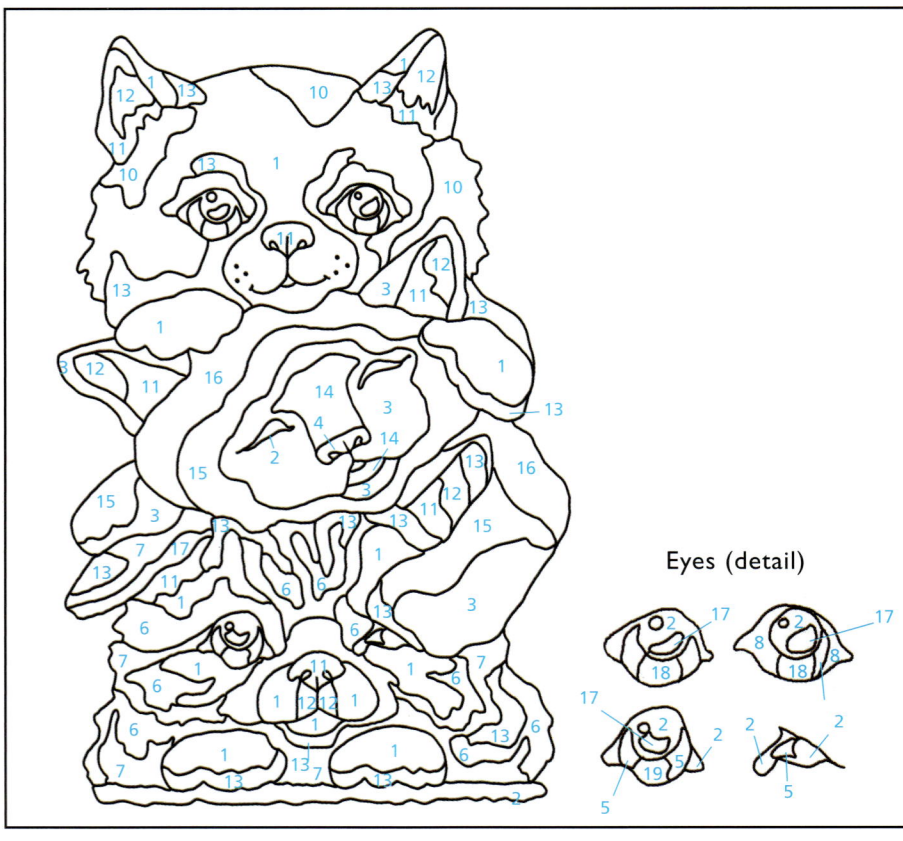

Eyes (detail)

Colors
1. White
2. Black
3. Shading Flesh
4. Raw Umber
5. Yellow Green
6. Grey Sky
7. Slate Grey
8. Calypso Blue
9. Granite
10. Camel/White 1:1
11. Raspberry/White 1:2
12. Raspberry/White 1:3
13. Grey Sky/White 1:1
14. Shading Flesh/Light Cinnamon 1:1
15. Shading Flesh/White 1:1
16. Antique White/White 1:1
17. Slate Grey/Graphite 1:1
18. Calypso Blue/White 1:1
19. Yellow Green/White 1:1

Meow

Palette
White
Black
Blush Flesh
Olive Green
Calypso Blue
Cadmium Orange
Cadmium Yellow
Lavender
Cadmium Red
Medium Flesh
Gingerbread
Grey Sky

Instructions
1. Trace drawing and transfer to paint surface.
2. Follow the diagram and paint areas as indicated.
3. Add outlines using Black Ultra Fine Point Sharpie as shown in picture.

Colors
1. White
2. Black
3. Blush Flesh
4. Olive Green/White 1:1
5. Calypso Blue/White 2:1
6. Cadmium Orange/Cadmium Yellow 1:1
7. Cadmium Orange/Cadmium Yellow/White 1:1:1
8. Lavender/White 1:1
9. Lavender/White 2:1
10. Cadmium Red/White 1:2
11. Calypso Blue/White 1:1
12. Cadmium Red/White 1:1
13. Medium Flesh/Gingerbread 1:1
14. Gingerbread
15. Grey Sky/White 1:1
16. Medium Flesh/White 1:3
17. Medium Flesh

57

Spoiled Rotten Dogs

Palette
Black
White
Slate Grey
Grey Sky
True Red
Deep Burgundy
Burnt Sienna
Medium Flesh
Cinnamon
Honey Brown
Camel
Sapphire
Raspberry
Buttermilk

Instructions
1. Trace drawing and transfer to paint surface.
2. Follow the diagram and paint areas as indicated.
3. Paint large areas of eye such as iris and pupil and add White highlights last.
4. Paint teeth #1 White.
5. Add dot of #1 White to nose on first and third dogs.
6. Add dot of #22 Raspberry mixture to corners of eyes on second and third dogs.
7. Use Black Ultra Fine Point Sharpie for saying, painting "DOGS" using Sapphire.
8. Use Black Ultra Fine Point Sharpie or Black paint and liner brush to add outlining as shown in picture.

Colors
1. White
2. Black
3. Slate Grey/Black 1:1
4. Slate Grey
5. Grey Sky
6. Grey Sky/White
7. True Red
8. Deep Burgundy
9. Burnt Sienna
10. Medium Flesh
11. Cinnamon
12. Cinnamon/Medium Flesh 1:1
13. Honey Brown/Camel 1:1
14. Honey Brown
15. Medium Flesh/Camel/White 1:1:1
16. Camel/White 1:2
19. Sapphire
20. Raspberry
21. Raspberry/Buttermilk 1:1
22. Raspberry/Buttermilk 1:2

Spoiled Rotten Cats

Palette

Black
White
Cadmium Red
Raspberry
Kelly Green
Yellow Green
Cadmium Yellow

Sapphire
Light Cinnamon
Shading Flesh
Antique White
Medium Flesh
Grey Sky

Instructions

1. Trace drawing and transfer to paint surface.
2. Follow the diagram and paint areas as indicated.
3. Paint large areas of eye such as iris and pupil and add White highlights last.
4. Use Black Ultra Fine Point Sharpie to add outlining as shown in picture.
5. Add three small dots to each side of muzzles using Black Sharpie.
6. Paint saying using Cadmium Red and Sapphire as shown in picture.

Colors

1. White
2. Black
3. Cadmium Red
4. Raspberry
5. Kelly Green
6. Yellow Green
7. Cadmium Yellow
8. Sapphire
9. Raspberry/White 1:2
10. Raspberry/White 1:1
11. Light Cinnamon
12. Shading Flesh
13. Shading Flesh/White 1:1
14. Antique White/White 1:1
15. Antique White/White 1:2
16. Medium Flesh
17. Medium Flesh/White 1:2
18. Medium Flesh/White 2:1
19. Grey Sky/White 1:1

Eyes (detail)

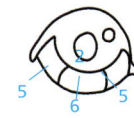

SPOILED ROTTEN CATS LIVE HERE

🐾 ALPHABETS 🐾

A B C D E F G H I J K L M
N O P Q R S T U V W X Y
Z 1 2 3 4 5 6 7 8 9 0

a b c d e f g h i j k l m n o
p q r s t u v w x y z

TENNIS BALL ALPHABET

A B C D E F G H I
J K L M N O P Q R
S T U V W X Y Z

1 2 3 4 5 6 7 8 9 0

a b c d e f g h i j k
l m n o p q r s t u
v w x y z

I LOVE MY

Produced by:
Kooler Design Studio, Inc.
399 Taylor Blvd., Suite 104
Pleasant Hill, CA 94523
info@koolerdesign.com

Production Team:
- Artist: Linda Gillum
- Creative Director: Donna Kooler
- Editor-In-Chief: Judy Swager
- Senior Graphic Designer: Ashley Rocha
- Photographer: Dianne Woods
- Art Director: Basha Kooler

Published by:
Copyright ©2008 by Leisure Arts, Inc.,
5701 Ranch Drive, Little Rock, AR 72223
www.leisurearts.com

We have made every effort to ensure that these instructions are accurate and complete. We cannot, however, be responsible for human error, typographical mistakes or variation in individual work. This publication is protected under federal copyright laws. Reproduction or distribution of this publication or any other Leisure Arts publication, including publications which are out of print, is prohibited unless specifically authorized. This includes, but is not limited to, any form of reproduction or distribution on or through the internet, including posting, scanning, or e-mail transmission.